My Life as a Foreign Country

Brian Turner

My Life as a Foreign Country

JONATHAN CAPE
LONDON

Published by Jonathan Cape 2014

2 4 6 8 10 9 7 5 3 1

First published in Great Britain in 2014 by
Jonathan Cape
Random House, 20 Vauxhall Bridge Road,
London SW1V 2SA

www.vintage-books.co.uk

Addresses for companies within
The Random House Group Limited can be found at:
www.randomhouse.co.uk/offices.htm

The Random House Group Limited Reg. No. 954009

A CIP catalogue record for this book is available from the British Library

ISBN 9780224097437

The Random House Group Limited supports the Forest Stewardship
Council® (FSC®), the leading international forest-certification organisation. Our
books carrying the FSC label are printed on FSC®-certified paper. FSC is the only
forest-certification scheme supported by the leading environmental organisations,
including Greenpeace. Our paper procurement policy can be found at
www.randomhouse.co.uk/environment

Typeset in Miller Text by Palimpsest Book Production Ltd, Falkirk, Stirlingshire

Printed and bound in Germany by GGP Media GmbH, Pößneck

My
Life
as a
Foreign
Country

I am a drone aircraft plying the darkness above my body, flying over my wife as she sleeps beside me, over the curvature of the earth, over the glens of Antrim and the Dalmatian coastline, the shells of Dubrovnik and Brčko and Mosul arcing in the air beside me, projectiles filled with poems and death and love.

I am 32,000 feet over the Atlantic seaboard. The fields, the orchards, the woodlands below press together the way countries on maps do, coursing waterways, paved roads and dirt tracks and furrows cutting through. Countries touching countries. Bosnia and Vietnam and Iraq and Northern Ireland and Korea and Russia pressed together in the geography below. Cumulus scattered above them, their shapes authored by sunlight on the ground beneath. The Battle of Guadalcanal emerges from the shadows where my grandfather lives. Now Bougainville. Guam. Iwo Jima.

Highway 1 – Iraq's Highway of Death – stretches through desert on one side and California's San Joaquin Valley on the other. The eucalyptus trees of my childhood line the sides of the highway. In places I can see the scorch marks on the asphalt where transport trucks were left to burn. My dead Uncle Paul steals oranges in the night groves there, just as he did when I was eight years old, while fresh dark earth covers the newly dead on the other side of the highway. Owls perch on their gravestones calling out for water.

Each night I do this, monitoring heat signatures in the landscape, switching from white-hot to black-hot lenses as I bank and turn, gathering circuit by circuit the necessary intelligence, all that I have done, all that we have done, compressed into the demarcations in the map below.

'Here's the situation,' Sergeant First Class Fredrickson said, gesturing to the tiny plastic red and blue flags driven into the ground on thin metal poles. There must have been thirty or forty of them arrayed in the grass around us, in no discernible pattern. It was September 2003, and, like some of the others gathered around SFC Fredrickson on that clipped green field outside our classroom, I'd been scanning the scene to gauge what the flags might represent. On the big-screen television in the company dayroom, the war waited for us. Fighters who shot at American soldiers in Baghdad and Samarra and Tikrit were perfecting their trigger squeeze for us.

'We are surrounded by the dead. And by parts of the dead,' Fredrickson said, emphasising the word *parts*. 'Your unit has come upon the scene of a possible ambush. Everybody's dead. This is not a mass casualty exercise. So. What's the first thing we should do?'

One of the students in the back said, 'We better start scrounging up a shitload of body bags.'

Fredrickson smiled.

'No. Like everything else, the first thing you do, the *first* thing: set up security. Create a perimeter, and then you can get to work.' He went on to explain that a certain number of soldiers would be needed to deal with the task at hand, especially if time was of the essence, as it always was in these situations. 'You'll want to photograph the scene from several angles, if you have a digital camera and if you have the time. That's why the flags are here. You have to place one flag at the spot of each body, or body *part*, that you find. If you don't have a camera, do a field sketch.' We practice drawing hasty field sketches in our pocket notebooks, creating small legends in the margins, crossed lines with tiny arrowheads: a rough guide to the cardinal directions.

He tells us to use a certain Department of Defense form to label and keep track of the dead sealed up in their body bags. 'And remember, this is very important: never place two separated parts into the same bag.' He pauses. 'I'll give you an example.' He points to the nearest soldier and tells him to lie down and act like he's dead.

Sgt Gordon kneels on the damp grass and then lies down prostrate, with his right arm stretched out from his side, as if pointing to something beyond us. His mouth is open and at first he stares blankly at the few clouds above. Then, he closes his eyes and assumes the role of the dead.

A few of us joke about Gordon and his ability to sham, to loaf, no matter the circumstances as Fredrickson steps closer to the body. 'Imagine that this arm,' he says, gesturing toward Gordon's outstretched limb, 'has been blown off, here at the armpit. And there's no other body nearby, and you can plainly see that it's the same uniform and everything. Still, you have to put his body in one bag and give it a number and then you have to put this arm in another bag with a different number.' He looks across our faces. 'Don't assume anything. They'll figure it out back home. They'll test for DNA and all that jazz.' A pause, and then he continues: 'Let me tell you something – you don't want to be the one who makes some poor family bury their soldier with somebody else's body part. Roger that?'

As he carries on explaining the work at hand, my eyes wander over the grassy field and the bright flags stationed in the earth around us. It's a rare day of sun in Ft Lewis, Washington state, and the early morning light illuminates the translucent nature of the grass in its subtle gesture toward infinity. The dead assume their positions. Some of them lie on their sides, others rest on their backs, their faces lifted toward the sky. Each with a numbered flag beside him. Some turn their heads slowly toward me, their eyes crossed over into the landscape of clouds as they call out with hoarse voices, quietly, asking for a drink of water. A small sip, they say. Just a sip of water.

The 1st Platoon of Blackhorse Company sits on the tile floor of the weight room cleaning weapons with CLP and bore snakes and dental tools after running lanes in the woods and conducting live-fire exercises. The men are dirty and exhausted. They laugh and shout out their orders as bags of burritos are delivered from the twenty-four-hour Taco Bell off post. I'm in the adjacent room with my squad leader, Staff Sergeant Bruzik, and Sergeant Zapata, my fellow team leader. We watch more of the war on television. Several Marines rush under fire to a bridge in Nasiriyah, Iraq.

They crawl on the concrete and asphalt of the roadway as the invisible trails of bullets zip past them from the far shore of the river. They return fire, shooting at what I've been trained to think of as *known and suspected enemy targets*. The Marines rush the bridge over and over as the newscast replays the scene.

The television is on mute. I don't know what Bruzik and Zapata are thinking, but I'm looking at the far shore and trying to make out the muzzle flashes. Those on the other side of the river are honing the same fundamentals of marksmanship we've studied at the rifle ranges of Ft Lewis. It isn't something I mention to Bruzik and Zapata. I feel remote, somewhat cold, my mind working out the possible trajectories that might bring me home. I'm Sgt Turner and I'm a team leader preparing to deploy to combat. But there's something echoing through the branches and channels of my central nervous system.

On the other side of that river, Iraqis continue to crouch along walls and lie on rooftops in the prone. Even when I fall asleep tonight, they'll continue to fire their weapons. The news anchor will narrate the action. On replay. Figures in the distance. Soldiers running toward the bridge. The sight picture placed over them as I dream and sleep in the state of Washington. The Iraqi men, again and again, pulling the trigger.

3

Once the plane comes to a stop in the dry waves of heat and the orange night air of Kuwait, we're bussed north to one of the many camps along the border with Iraq. The military supply system begins delivering a staggering amount of new equipment to my unit. We shuffle through three different sight systems for our carbines until settling on a sight we're told Special Forces use, too. Among other things, I am given a coil of metal with an eyepiece at one end and a tiny optical instrument at the other – for snaking under a door and peering into a room. Journalists report of units lacking the proper gear, like body armor for flak vests and slat armor for Humvees or five-ton trucks; we are given so much new and expensive equipment that our unit has to stow much of it away in metal connexes, the large cargo boxes used by the military to ship much of its inventory. I am in the first Stryker brigade to deploy to combat and the path of a number of careers depends upon how lethal and how durable this unit will be during its time in-country – maybe that's why we're getting special attention. Our Strykers weigh nineteen tons and are fitted with wheels rather than the tracks of traditional armored personnel carriers; soon local Iraqis will refer to us as *the ghosts* because of the speed and silence of our approach. When we learn about this, our platoon sergeant, SFC Daigle, changes our platoon nickname from The Bonecrushers to The Ghostriders. My new call sign: Ghost 1–3 Alpha.

SSG Kaha, who will later go AWOL, packs away some of this equipment when I pass him on my way to the showers. He's been fired from his job as squad leader due to perceived incompetence. I nod as he continues to sing 'Raindrops Keep Falling on My Head'. Long after dusk has shifted to stars, I lie back on my bunk and think about the divorce paperwork signed a few months earlier, the few addresses where I might mail a letter if I were to write one, and it occurs to me that if I were to die in the country north of our camp during the year ahead, my death wouldn't irreparably alter the life of another. My address is now my Name, Rank, Unit, and the last four digits of my social security number are stenciled in black spray paint onto the duffel bag containing my worldly goods. It doesn't seem possible that in the years to come, in the years after the war, I'll get married and move across country and start my life over. Why should it seem plausible? No one stood at the unit staging area in Ft Lewis to wish me goodbye and, however I make it home, in a body bag, on a gurney or stepping off onto the tarmac with my duffel in the belly of the plane, no one will be there to welcome me home.

I step outside the tent to get a breath of air and quiet. A slight breeze lifts fine grains of sand from the landscape of the desert as if a white gossamer veil were slowly being drawn over the surface of the earth. There is a distinct sense of the past and the future being erased at the horizon's edge. The circumference of the world retracts itself until it comes to a rest beneath the nightfall of stars within my field of vision.

Later tonight, I will read a book, a translation of *Meditations* by Marcus Aurelius. I will think about the idea of home, what the country before me might have in store, and know that I have become, as Aurelius had quoted centuries before, one of the many 'leaves that the wind drives earthward'.

The sand under our feet has turned to a fired-brick orange after a night of rain. Soldiers cluster in small groups up and down the column of several hundred vehicles in a loggerhead formation, waiting for the word, waiting to roll out. Smoking Marlboro 100s and unfiltered Camels, army coffee steaming from the metal canteen cups in their hands. And as we prepare to head north, I remembered these words:

> Facing us in the field of battle are teachers, fathers and sons; / grandsons, grandfathers, wives' brothers; mothers' brothers / and fathers of wives.

We lock and load our weapons, mount up and move out.

It is 3 December 2003. Our first day in Iraq. We are traveling roughly 480 km to our new home north of Baghdad: Firebase Eagle. From build-up through deployment – from Herodotus to Xenophon, from Cornelius Ryan to Lieutenant General Harold G. Moore – I am aware of a variety of insertion narratives. As a boy, I was fascinated by historical accounts which followed the trail of Custer's cavalry in 1876, from the quartermaster's logistics that supplied the campaign to the mule skinners and scouts and newspapermen who accompanied Custer into the Battle of the Greasy Grass, otherwise known as the Battle of the Little Bighorn.

We know our prelude will be different from the trenches of the First World War or the front lines of Korea. We won't hear the battle in progress and work our way toward it as baggage trains of wounded, exhausted soldiers and civilians carrying their lives on their backs travel in the opposite direction. Our battle space – and perhaps it's a cliché now – will occur in a 360-degree, three-dimensional environment. When we entered this desert, the available calculus involved in the creation of any new moment changed. Anything is possible. A dead farm animal on the shoulder of the road could harbor an improvised bomb sewn into its belly. A bullet might ride the cool currents between one human being and another. A Hellcat missile or a wire-guided Tow missile might rend the moment open.

A few hours in, my squad leader needed a break. He'd been up in the forward hatch, in the full blast of the desert wind and engine exhaust, since early that morning. I covered for him, took over in the hatch for a while. Our Stryker was the lead vehicle for the entire convoy. Behind me – nearly 3,500 soldiers. In front of me – Iraq, history, combat. We rode on a war elephant made of steel. Blackhawk helicopters escorted us from their stations in the sky.

Up ahead: an old white- and orange-paneled beat-up

sedan parked on the left shoulder of the road. On the opposite side of the road and walking through a thin vegetation of desert scrubland, four men, all dressed in jeans and thin black jackets, one with a lightly checked *shemagh* wrapped loosely around his neck. Four men in civilian clothes walking single file and evenly spaced, the way soldiers do, each trying to conceal an AK-47 by holding it against the far side of their bodies as they crossed the road.

They didn't stop. I pointed my M4 at them. I belted out a series of linked obscenities and the Stryker bore down on them. My thumb had already flipped the selector lever on my weapon from *safe* to *semi* and all the moment needed were the bullets I was leaning in to sight on the medium-sized man, second from the left, the one with the potbelly. The sight's center dot, small and red, the premonition of an entry wound, focused right about where his first or second rib curved beneath his coat. My finger in the trigger housing.

The world disappeared around those four men and their car the way house lights in a theater go dark, a spotlight focusing in on the killer and those about to be killed. I pressed the weapon deeper into my shoulder and exhaled.

Parazoo, our vehicle commander, broke in over the intercom – 'Badge! I got a badge!'

He was below, watching the moment unfold through a gun-mount camera. That shout, that fraction of a second, saved the man's life. He was a civilian contractor (a mercenary in any other war). And the man to the left of him, the man who wore a shiny badge hanging from a black cord around his neck – he was from Chicago.

5

In a museum in Kyoto, Japan, years later, I find myself mesmerised by an oil painting of an archer. He kneels to stretch a bow fully back, an arrow poised at the moment of flight. There is a wall made of cloth behind him. The branch of a cherry tree, at the end of its bloom, bends into the frame. The archer shows no sign of strain, despite the tension of the bow. He simply gazes forward at something out of view. Maybe there is a target and maybe there isn't. The painting doesn't show us. That's not the point. The point is to become one with the moment. To meld with the motion of the instrument. To become the archer and the bow combined.

6

Firebase Eagle is an hour's drive north of Baghdad, set among farmland and orchards, just south of the winding

Tigris River. Unlike the dry, flat, barren solitude of the desert I'd expected, there are eucalyptus groves, water buffalo, stands of sunflower grown six feet tall and swaying overhead for a quarter of a mile or more. In the winter mornings a thick fog rolls off the Tigris just like it does back home in California, in the vineyards and olive groves along the San Joaquin River.

It's a fairly small base, housing our company, the outgoing company and some Military Police on a few acres at most. It's horseshoe-shaped, like a donut with a bite taken out of one side. The perimeter of the base is formed by large earthen berms fixed with concertina wire, punctuated by two-story-high concrete towers set at intervals. A huge metal gate swings open to allow convoys in and out – vehicles that must, once out, negotiate a chicane as the dirt road snakes its way to the main paved road into the town of Balad. Between the front gate and the paved civilian road is a distance of eighty meters, and here exists a tiny shantytown we call the Hajji Market.

We're allowed to walk in groups outside the gate in order to shop. We can buy a plate of grilled lamb and seasoned rice, wash it down with a little Fanta. Haggle with the vendors over souvenirs, mostly, like the cheap, flat black throwing knives which we fling at the trunks of palm trees to whittle away our boredom. We buy Iraqi flags and Iranian money and pirated movies on cheap discs for a buck each. In the market, we can procure European porn videos and Iraqi bayonets and even talk the vendors into driving to Baghdad for an acoustic guitar if we really want one. Velour rugs with beautiful women's faces stitched into them are rolled up and bound with twine, carried over the buyer's shoulder as he walks back into the firebase.

My platoon is quartered inside a long rectangular building once used as an Iraqi army barracks. Slogans are painted on the walls in large Arabic script – colorful paintings of tanks, soldiers and crews standing bravely beside them. We sleep under these slogans and paintings in our green sleeping bags, puss-pads beneath us – thin rolls of foam for some, thin air mattresses for others – softening the concrete and breaking the winter chill seeping up through the foundations.

It is cramped, with soldiers and their gear piled side by side, allowing only a narrow aisle from one end of the room to the other. A couple of portable heaters stationed equidistant along the center aisle. But it feels *safe* inside this building. The walls are thick and can withstand the shelling. Unlike the rest of the platoons in the company – who arguably have much nicer living quarters, housed by threes and fours in heated metal trailers that the mortar shrapnel can easily chew through – I think we've been given a sturdy place to sleep and prep for our missions.

In a very short time, a few days at most, America

disappears. Its streets and cities drift and fade away; they are replaced by orchards and date groves and the Tigris, by an Iraqi countryside in a time of violence.

7

We are shelled on close to a daily basis.

The unit we are replacing has been stationed at Firebase Eagle as part of the initial invasion and is now preparing to go home. So those we fight have what's called a *target rich environment*. In military parlance: the enemy is bracketing our position. Basically, an Iraqi mortar crew is, day by day and round by round, discovering the proper distance, elevation, deflection and explosive charge necessary to fire rounds directly into our camp. Yesterday, it was a round exploding one hundred meters south of the camp perimeter. Today three or four fall roughly one hundred meters north of the camp's front gate. If they adjust correctly, there's a good chance mortar rounds will explode inside the wire tomorrow. It's a matter of ballistics, range, velocity.

And patience. It's a matter of great patience.

8

The mortar crew has locked on to us and is now beginning to *fire for effect*. The sound of the detonations, the crack and airy breath of it all. Sometimes a distinct explosion. Other times the rounds land nearly simultaneously with an over-whelming, godlike finality, the soft architecture of the brain registering each concussion as a type of conversation. The extension of an idea expressed in the physical language of shrapnel, fear: someone is hunting for your soul.

9

Our best bet is to triangulate their firing points. My squad searches for the craters where the rounds landed. Farm dogs bark in the distance. The tac lights on our weapons dimly illuminate the scene as we crouch over one of the holes to conduct a crater analysis – noting dirt kicked up by the explosion, placing small sticks across the length and width of the crater, and then determining a back azimuth with a compass held in the palm and sighted down the course of one of the sticks, the needle trembling under the glass as it points into the darkness. This is supposed to lead us to the enemy. So we send out counter-mortar patrols to try to locate the men we call Ali Baba, but Ali Baba is a ghost. Ali Baba has disappeared into the orchards and orange groves. Ali Baba sleeps with his wife under layers of thick blankets and roofing and clouds the moon cannot break through. Ali Baba dreams of green rolling fields where American soldiers lie down and pretend they are dead. Small numbered flags driven into the ground beside them.

10

Sgt Zapata wore headphones connected to the mine detector in his hands, which hovered two to three inches over the soil, reflecting the moonlight falling through the bare trees of the orchard. His squad automatic weapons gunner, Liu, pulled security as the mine detector swept from right to left and back again, pausing here and there as Zapata listened for all that might be buried in the earth. Liu stood with a small, foldable shovel in one hand and the barrel of his weapon pointed up at the planet Mars. He mulled over which type of bumper to buy for the '67 Shelby he had stored in the garage of his parents' home back in San Francisco.

I was in the animal stall with the prisoners: all the men from the adjacent farmhouses who were of military age. We'd cinched their hands behind their backs, the flex-cuffs binding their wrists together. Pulled sandbags over their heads. We'd walked them in a silent line from their homes and across the dirt courtyard; the women and children were gathered together in one of the front rooms of the biggest house, given blankets to keep themselves warm, a guard standing in the doorway to watch over them as their homes were thoroughly searched. In the animal stall, each man was separated a few paces from the other prisoners and made to place the instep of one foot over the heel of the opposite leg before being guided down into a kneeling position in the loose straw at the center of the enclosure.

The morning call to Azan wouldn't happen for another two or three hours. For now, we leaned in close to the hooded men and whispered into their ears the words we most wanted to hear from them – *How-wyn, motherfucker? How-wyn?**

The sergeant to my right was stuck on repeat, circling a prisoner. 'You know, don't you? Yeah. You know. You know. I know you fucking know. Squirrely little bastard. But it's all right, all you gotta do is tell. Tell us what you know.' The muzzle of his carbine rested against the man's back.

A milk cow stared at us with its huge brown eyes. The milk cow tilted its head from one side to the other, then lowered its mouth and nostrils to snuff its breath in quickly and blast a short snort of air into the straw, which rose in a cloud of dust and paper-thin husks. Another soldier called out from the haystack in the corner, 'I got nothing here, Sergeant. You

---

* *Mortars? Mortars?*

want me to keep looking?' The sergeant seemed to ignore the question. Instead, he leaned closer to the hooded man in the straw before him: 'You want me to have him keep looking? Why don't you just tell us instead?'

Hours later, when the dawn breaks over the far mountains, some higher-up will realise we've raided the wrong site, and that the target house is actually beyond the date palms across the river. We'll have to remove the hoods from these men, gingerly cut the flex-cuffs with the saw-toothed blades of our Leathermans, and then shake their hands, bowing to them slightly, apologising, constantly, holding our black-gloved palms out to them, 'We're sorry; we're so sorry, *sadiq*, but . . . My apologies . . . I'm really . . .' and so on as we back up, mount our vehicles and roll out.

But for the time being, I stood in the animal stall and studied the bound men slumping forward in the straw. The night wore on. Most of them shivered in the cold, one of them sobbing to himself, while in the front room of the large farmhouse another soldier stared through night-vision goggles at the women and children huddled in a black corner. They whispered to one another, hushing the sleepless children in their laps. And the soldier in the doorway traversed the room with his left eye in a luminous globe, that insomniac green, the color of fresh leaves lit from within, and he stopped his gaze on a woman staring directly back at him, whose eyes reflected in bright ovals of phosphorescent green, so clear the soldier quickly turned away, shuffled, spat a stream of tobacco juice into the hallway, cleared his throat.

In the orchard rows beyond, Liu continued to think of San Francisco and Ford Mustangs while Sgt Zapata paused with the search coil of the metal detector over a slight depression, closed his eyes and listened to the earth.

11

Those bovine eyes in the animal stall. They make me think of a Scottish isle, halfway between Gairloch and Ullapool, during my grandfather's war, cold waters of the Minch in the distance, the occasional ship steeling itself to Stornoway, where a flock of sheep, eighty-strong, graze among the emptied houses of men. In a land where people are few to begin with, there are none here any longer.

It creates unease among the sheep, who stand in the hard wind both day and night, buffeted, the conversations among them understood in the angle of the head, the slow blink of the eyes.

And how could they have seen this coming, even in a world where the slaughterhouse waits in the end for each of them, how could they have known this?

When the bombs burst with an alien, mechanical sound, the sheep bolt in the muscle, tethers holding them taut in place while the brownish, aerosol cloud of anthrax begins to drift its spores toward them.

There is only so much pain a body can withstand, only so much undoing. Within days, they begin to die.

This was recorded by scientists, on 16mm color film. This is history. It really happened. You can see it for yourself. You can watch their jaws mouthing upward toward God.

12

Because of the mud, which could easily become a soupy quagmire and impassable for heavy vehicles and soldiers alike, the engineers constructing the camp laid down a bed of gravel. They also constructed massive concrete blast walls, known as 'T-walls', to cordon off sleeping areas, walls meant to contain the spray of shrapnel. But the blast walls weren't lined high with sandbags. So, when a mortar round exploded in Firebase Eagle during this period, it not only sent out mortar shrapnel but lifted a lethal spray of gravel from the roadbed. Compounding the problem, the T-walls could act as ricochet walls – deflecting shrapnel and other flying debris toward someone who might not have been killed or wounded otherwise, someone who would normally be considered out of the blast radius.

It is like living inside a sleeping bomb.

Firebase Eagle wraps its horseshoe around an Iraqi family
with their children and goats and chickens; they live in a small
compound hidden by trees and an old derelict building. I
spend ten minutes consoling one of the elderly women living
there. With angry hand gestures she explains to me through
the wire fence that an incoming mortar round meant to kill
guys like me has, in fact, strayed into her yard, nearly killing
her and her grandchildren. And she's angry about the chickens.
She argues her case for compensation for the two dead birds
now obliterated in her yard. Her hands rise and fall as she
speaks: I imagine a burst of plumage rising over the yard
before the feathers drift down in slow arcs of light and shadow,
as if tracing the waning surface of a gibbous moon. On behalf
of the United States Government, I am able to use a mixture
of English and broken Arabic to negotiate and compensate
her family for their loss with the seven dollars I have on me
at the time.

I am in my desert fatigues. We don't call them fatigues. We
call them Desert Camouflage Uniforms. We call them DCUs.

And I have chambered a round – a NATO cartridge, 5.56mm bullet jacketed in brass. It's a round designed to yaw in soft tissue, and, at the right velocity, to cause hydraulic shock. For the time being, my selector lever is on *safe*, my right thumb resting on the lever. The dawn sun casts the sides of the village in a warm and sandy ochre, a warmth that causes rough-furred dogs to lift their heads and sniff the air, some of them beginning to catch scent of us.

We crouch beside a wall as my squad leader points to the target house. 'Take your team in through that door,' he whispers, motioning across a vacant stretch of earth to a dull metal door set at the front of the dwelling – 'right there.'

I run with the barrel of my M4 pointing the way forward. Adrenaline mutes the world around me until all I can hear is the sound of my own breathing, gear jostling on my flak vest, the dull clanging of ammunition strapped to my chest, impossibly loud, so loud I think the dogs will bark and the people inside will bolt upright from sleep, Bruzik disappearing behind me as the world funnels in toward the door, my desert boots slapping the hardpan.

I lift the muzzle of the weapon as I kick in the door and I bring it down, eye-level, instinctual, my index finger poised over its trigger.

Drizzling rain. Days and days of it.

Some of the prisoners stand huddled under a sheet of warped plywood, whispering in voices too low to hear. Others are sectioned off in different holding pens with no makeshift roof to shelter them. One of the most recent prisoners simply squats down wearing sandals and a light jacket over his *thawb* – what most of us at Firebase Eagle call a *man dress*. His hands are flex-cuffed behind his back, sandbag over his head.

There's another Iraqi standing off to the side, not far from where I pass by on my way to the internet station inside the battalion command post. Two weeks in, and I'm hoping to check email from back home before the platoon rolls out for another night's raid. But this second man is staring at me. It's a long, hard look he gives. I match him stare for stare, and the two of us just stand here, one moment in history's vast archive of the unrecorded, staring each other down. The rain picking up slightly as the wind drives its chill from north-west to south-east, from Anatolia to the Gulf.

We both live in pens made of wire. I carry an M4, have a boot knife strapped to my flak vest and the American flag silently listening in from the uniform patch on my shoulder.

He's in his man dress, wearing sandals and shivering in the damp cold. There's a sand-bagged guard shack at one corner of the holding area. I occasionally see military police shuffling a prisoner along one of the wire corridors and to a green plastic port-o-let, but normally the MPs stay in that shack to keep warm and bullshit about things going on back home, about girlfriends, football, the latest rumor or *word – What's the word? Any word yet?*

16

Saddam Hussein was captured during Operation Red Dawn on 14 December 2003. I remember it well. I watched streams of brilliant tracer-fire arc over the farmlands and across the river that night. I listened to the celebration. And, in the morning, I put on my boots and lightly oiled the bolt of my weapon and I returned to work, just as the mortar crews bracketing Firebase Eagle returned to theirs.

17

I am afraid much of the time. Deep-down scared. Afraid so long and continually that it becomes normal and I don't even realise I'm scared. I'm worried I'll end up in pieces with little flags pinned into the ground beside me. I'm worried I'll be blinded or crippled. I'm worried the same might happen to one of the guys in the squad – to Fiorillo or Jax or Gigantor or Knight or Liu or Noodles or Z or Zoo or Whit or Bruzik. And that it'll be my fault. That I'll make a mistake. One quick and misguided decision that I'll have to live with for the rest of my life, or else lie in my grave, dismantled by it.

18

I begin to imagine a landscape of ghosts. The way photographers talk about the presence of the dead on the battlefield at Gettysburg. How their shadows fall among the leaves of grass and the stalks of purple thistleweed in the early morning light of Antietam, beyond the sunken road and in Miller's cornfield. Mayre's Heights at Fredricksburg, where the Union troops fell in vast waves. The dead at Agincourt and Senlac Hill. The trenches of the Somme. The beachhead at Anzac Cove. Ghosts lying under the leafed-out trees along the Chickahominy River. Vicksburg. Cold Harbor.

As I gaze out over the morning mist coming off the Tigris, near a spot where army engineers have spanned the river with a pontoon bridge, the more recent dead from the strafed and bombed Highway 1 cross the bridge and disappear into the eucalyptus grove beyond. Some of them pause in the crosshatching of branches and leaves to look back, the mist a kind of smoke rising from their shoulders and heads as they consider the months and years stretching behind them.

19

The shitters – what we call our line of port-o-lets – are so foul and backed up that the company first sergeant places a guard on them: the guard ordered to inspect each toilet immediately after a soldier has used it.

Nearby, Jax leans against a Humvee and talks about Arizona, his voice drifting into the dusk as I focus on the trunk of a nearby date palm. With each cutting throw of the knife, I carve my name into its elephant hide. The air is tinged with the smell of diesel exhaust, trashfires, and excrement. Fiorillo lights a cigarette and hands the pack to Bruzik.

Artillery hammers the evening from a distant base.

20

I notice two prisoners inside the brick building where we house all the captured enemy weapons. I don't know why they are kept separate from the other prisoners in the main holding area outside, but I assume they are either high-value prisoners and must be quarantined from the others or, more likely, they have been forgotten within the vast machinery of war. They are caged in a tiny side room with a wall of evenly spaced iron bars sunk in the concrete foundation and buried in the ceiling plaster seven or eight feet above. Like something you might find in a jail cell in the American West, circa 1870. A ghost-town cell. Dark. Reeking of urine and human grime. I can barely make out the forms shivering shoulder to shoulder, squatting down, hunched, a couple of pieces of soaked cardboard the only thing between them and the cold concrete.

I can feel their eyes through the darkness. Looking at me. Chiseling into memory the anonymity of the uniform. They can barely distinguish me as a man, either.

21

We're driving past a market area, and our Iraqi interpreter says, 'From the same guy you can buy a porno disc and you can buy a religious disc. The pornos are stolen from satellite channels and recorded from the XXL channel – French channel. Very good one,' he says, blowing smoke from a Kent Premium 9 out of the air-guard hatch.

'Viagra, breast enlargements – you can get anything here. BDSM stuff. Lubricants. Even fake pussies.'

Fake pussies?

'Yeah. Fake pussies. Whatever you want.'

22

In the dream, the mortars explode in the same spot they hit only a couple of days ago – just beyond where I was sleeping in my hooch, my living quarters, the rounds detonating on the other side of the Hesco barriers set up to absorb the spray of shrapnel. I scramble to get out of my rack and grab my gear, but I'm stuck in the slow motion of dream; barefoot, pants on, shirtless – my head and body thrumming as the sound waves reverberate outward from the blast. And there's a white camel beside me, a gentle, shaggy-coated creature, white as the albino camel I've seen grazing on the bluffs beside the Tigris, near Bridge Number 4.

The camel swings its broad head to nudge me until I pitch forward, stumbling, my toes flexing to push off from the hard grit and launch forward, fully airborne, gliding in the momentum the camel has given me, drifting a couple of feet above the ground and stabilising, the white camel walking beside me as I hover. The camel is whispering some-thing, its voice at the twin thresholds of human hearing, low and ethereal all at once, a voice whispered from enormous lungs, from a rare creature, a guide to the landscape of dream, a creature I need to know, I think, as I continue to move the way sand is carried over the surface of the earth by wind, away from the detonations and the waves rippling outward, away from the soldiers sprinting in slow motion to overhead cover, away.

23

The company commander of the outgoing unit is killed in his hooch during a mortar attack. I'm promised by one of the sergeants from their unit, a man who talks with a rough shadow in his voice, that 'Tomorrow, I promise you, you watch – tomorrow there'll be two or three bodies right outside this gate.' And tomorrow is a day when the sun breaks through. Forsman wakes me up to tell me, to take me outside our hooch, outside the cold barracks, to show me. And Sergeant First Class Braddock stands there, too. Back home, Braddock and his wife go to art galleries on the weekends. They collect watercolors and drink German Rieslings from black-stemmed wine glasses made from the finest Austrian lead crystal. Forsman eats a Snickers. None of us says a word. Two palm trees cast their shade on the ground. Blue sky above. Flies buzzing around their heads. And a pool of blood. A couple of nineteen-year-old soldiers from the outgoing unit walk up and kick one of the dead men's feet. One of them says to that dead man's body, to all of us – *Last Call, motherfucker. Last Call.*

24

Pre-Islamic Arabs believed that if they were to die prematurely, in an unnatural or violent death, their owl-spirit would rise from the head at the time of death to perch on their grave. From atop their graves the owl would call out – 'Water, Water' – until the death was avenged. In a natural death, the spirit would remain in the household for a hundred years, watching over the family and offering news from the other side.

25

The mortar rounds – I hear the outgoing booms of their cannons, listen for the missiles spinning over the rooftops of the city, consider the deflection and elevation, windage applied by the breeze, the atmosphere's humidity, the covalent bonds within the molecules which constitute the air, the velocity of metal given an irrevocable intention.

And I wonder if people will one day gather around the

impact sites, as they did when I was Infantryman Turner, in Bosnia, a NATO peacekeeper at the end of the last century, kneeling beside the pitted and star-shaped asphalt and concrete, where brushes were dipped into buckets of red paint until the camel hair soaked full. Sarajevo roses they called them, the brushes pausing over the site for a brief moment before the arm completed its motion and the paint was pressed as deep into the explosion as the radius of the blast would allow.

And I remember how the ghosts wandered through the streets there, some gathering at the café where they died in the artillery barrage on an evening in May, others leaning on the railings of a bridge to watch the river glide and disappear under the arched span of stone as an ancient voice called out from a nearby minaret. I knelt beside their graves in a cemetery set in a grove of pines. On each stone, the faces of the dead were fixed in a brooch, their names inscribed into the white marble below.

Hooded crows perched on some of the headstones, cocking their heads from side to side, gauging the wind, yawning their beaks open and shut as the last of the day's light filtered down through the pine boughs.

I'd sometimes sit atop the metal connexes near the camp ammo point to view the bombed-out houses at the city's edge – the small ruined town of Brčko. The haze of trashfires drifted over in a noxious sweet perfume that partially obscured the houses, which emerged like a long row of broken skulls each morning. Nailed plastic sheets hung loose from their window frames, flapping in the breeze.

Fires burned in Mostar and Visegrád, Gradačac, Gorazde and Sarajevo. Season by season, the dead sank deeper into the soil – each enduring the severe and exacting labor of leaves and rain and sun in their compression of mineral and stone, there within the worm-driven kingdom of hunger, phyla of the blind.

26

Many of the bones of those executed in Srebrenica were shipped to laboratories in Sarajevo and Banja Luka for identification. Femurs and sternums and vertebrae in glass-sealed containers lying patiently in the dark of a storage room. Sometimes they would be taken out and placed on a stainless steel table, the camera flash ringing off the metal as a photographer gathered images of bone, clothing, personal effects. Each piece given a corresponding number. Itemising the loss, making it small enough to hold.

27

And still the rounds kept coming.

28

Three men sit wordless in a wooden johnboat.

The old man on the back bench cups his hand around a Casio watch before depressing the button with his thumb to illuminate the hour. The numbers float in a sea of blue light. He nods to the other two and then leans back to press an oar into the muddy bank, pushing out into the Tigris. They duck their heads beneath the leaning stalks of papyrus while the boat creaks and wobbles. It emerges from the thicket and out into the current.

Zaid and Malik lift their oars and dip the blades quietly into the water, with Zaid picking a slow and deliberate pace. The braying of a donkey can be heard from somewhere upriver. Malik leans toward his brother. 'Sounds like your Shada. Calling you back to bed.'

Their father shushes them: 'Row.'

Zaid yawns and gives his brother a look, though Malik can't decipher his expression in the dark. They paddle forward, staying close to the shoreline as the river curves and straightens and curves again. In the hold, buried under old nets and burlap sacks, fishing poles, bait and tackle boxes, an improvised mortar tube made of thick-gauge PVC pipe lies hidden with its assorted gear – and a simple kitchen clock; the high-explosive round fired in the approximate direction of the nearby American base when the clock ticks zero.

They row in silence now, Zaid thinking of the name he'll give to the child he felt kicking his palm through the smooth wall of Shada's stomach, how cool her belly was when he pressed the side of his head there to listen, how the world disappeared when he heard that underwater sound of the future moving inside her. And Malik leans into the rowing, fascinated by the machine of his body, how the muscles of his arms take to the task of rowing so that the separation of body and oar become a fiction, Malik closing his eyes to subtract the night sounds of the world around him, until all that exists are the blades of their oars slipping into the water, two brothers in unison, propelling the boat forward with such ease he thinks they could just keep rowing, hour after hour, down through Baghdad and beyond, through sunrise and sunfall until they reached the wide mouth of the sea, the lights of Basra glowing behind them as they rowed into the crests and hollows of the Persian Gulf, Malik standing high at stern and calling out into the salt spray, calling to the adventurers who traveled these waters before him, the adventurers to come, saying, 'I'm here world – Malik, as alive as anyone who has ever lived. Malik.'

He doubles back to the oar in his hands, the propulsion of water, the cannon. There will be no Persian Gulf tonight, no string of lights on the shore of a distant country, because Malik is headed into battle. And if he is alive, it is because nobody, but nobody, is allowed to fuck with him. Not the helicopters. Not the tanks. Not the machine guns. *Nobody.* And the cannon in this boat will make sure of it.

Their father sits still, now and then blowing a long breath into his cupped hands to warm them. He watches his sons rowing moment by moment closer to the site. He thinks about the round resting beneath his feet. The timer he will set to go off shortly after dawn. He'll make sure of that. But there's no way to know for certain where the path of the round will take it. He pictures the rocket at its highest point, suspended for a brief moment in the blue ether. He wonders if another man's son will have just woken from a dream as the round pitches over and begins its descent, spinning.

Something catches his eye in the darkness. 'Ahead,' he says in a low whisper, leaning closer to them. 'The thicket on the left. There.'

The recruiter's office was outfitted with swivel chairs, a framed photograph of the President, an old steel-cased tanker desk. The sallow-faced man had a dot matrix printer and a green polyester suit decorated with military ribbons. I could feel the warmth of the freshly printed list of options in my hands. There were particle-board partitions and fluorescent lighting – and a photo of a camouflaged patrol, stealthily crossing water, all muzzles and war paint and shadowy intent.

I pointed to the list and said the word *Infantry*.

I don't remember when I started digging – maybe when I was about eleven years old, just after my family moved from Fresno, California, and into the farmlands and cattle-range land beyond the San Joaquin River – but I remember standing in one of the partially excavated holes and pausing to watch a slow-moving flock of vultures pass over to the sun-burned foothills at the base of the high sierras, Yosemite, Ansel Adams country. Those dark birds rode the cycling thermals in silence, now and then shifting their stiff wings to bank and turn, the way vultures do, heavy and awkward, articulating an invisible column of air rising through the troposphere and into the blue ether above.

And I dug, blade by blade, shoveling my way through scratchy sandy loam and down into the hardpan. I dug until the foxholes measured roughly chest-high for a grown man. I improvised overhead cover to protect against indirect fire, the metallic trajectories of mortar rounds and artillery shells. Wooden sector stakes marked the left and right limits for each soldier. A shelf carved into the back wall for binoculars, map, compass, maybe a cup of coffee in the winter. Grenade sumps and earthen berms to shield the defenders from small arms fire. Each hole big enough to hold a casket. Each fighting position based on the dimensions I'd found in Dad's infantry field manuals. And as I worked through the morning and deeper into the earth, I wore his old National Guard uniform, with black combat boots laced up tight. My green rucksack loaded with leftover C-rats, as well as a p-38 can opener, collapsible dinnerware, candles, matches, a coiled length of nylon cordage, an emergency survival kit waterproofed in plastic, a mummy bag for inclement weather, *Penthouse* magazines from 1976 and *Soldier of Fortune*.

I signed the paper and joined the infantry for reasons I won't tell you, and for reasons I will. I signed the paper and joined the infantry because at some point in the hero's life the hero is supposed to say *I swear*. I joined because I hadn't signed up for the First Gulf War. I signed the paper and joined the infantry because I'd drunk Wild Turkey and puked my guts out on the streets of South Korea for a year after grad school. I joined because I wanted to go to jungle warfare school down in Panama – not because I wanted to fight in the jungle, but to sleep in a hammock under a canopy of plants and trees I couldn't name, the night's known stars shifted out of place. I joined the infantry because I knew, even then, that most of what I've just said is total bullshit, or that it really won't answer a thing.

The first time my mother saw my father was in the summertime and he was on the local evening news. The anchor described the scene as they aired black and white footage taken earlier that afternoon.

A drunk driver in a pickup swerved into Dad's lane and side-swiped him as he rode his chopper down Chestnut

Avenue. I remember the first time he described his memories. After the crush of metal, after the clamping of brakes, the truck slid off into the near distance, and he found himself lying on his side in the middle of the road. The blacktop was scorching. And in the August heat the world assumed a tilted quality – the way a frame breaks and the photograph it holds slips at an angle from its station within. In my memory of that moment, his abdomen split open and his intestines spilled out onto the asphalt. Steam rose from that tissue and fluid as he lay in the broiling heat.

On the newscast, the anchor detailed the accounts of eyewitnesses who saw the driver of the truck stumble out of the cab once it had lurched to a halt. He'd gathered empty cans of cocktail mixer littering the seat of his truck and then carefully began placing them in a line from Dad's wrecked motorcycle to the front bumper of his truck, some distance away. When the police questioned him a short time later (and before he'd had a chance to sober up) the driver explained that those empty cocktail cans were visible proof of how Dad had been drinking while riding the chopper that now lay in ruins.

When I was a boy, he often went barefoot with cutoff jeans and no shirt, a can of Coors in his hand. The accident left a vertical pink scar, thick as a sword blade; the scar ran from the arrow-shaped point of the xiphoid process at the bottom of the sternum straight down to his belly button. He never had to say a word about it. The scar said it all. The scar said he could take it. Pain. Hardship. Trouble. The world could carve him open and spill his guts out, raw and steaming on the summer asphalt, and he could take it all. Come back up cussing and drinking and punching any doctors who got too close. The scar said – that which is written in the flesh is irrefutable. This is the mark of a man. *This* is what it takes.

33

The dojo – a space for martial artists to study and refine their art – represents *the place of the way*. In structural terms it is a kind of static space, in that it remains fixed to a specific location, and yet the space itself serves as both sanctuary and pathway. In this respect, it is similar to the human mind, fixed within the casing of the brain and yet the senses guide the world into the landscape of the mind, where each of us experiences our finite journey. The *kamidana*, or god-shelf, watches over the dojo from high up on the sensei's wall, which is considered the front of the dojo. And from this high altar, the gods receive devotions of worship in the form of fruit or water, bright flowers clipped from their stems. All bow as they enter and as they leave.

My dad converted our garage into a dojo. There were hand-crafted weights and pulleys for stretching, ingeniously built. He mounted a metal arm with a rotating hand to a floor-to-ceiling beam, an arm he'd welded from scrap metal and polished himself – simply to practice wrist locks and breakaways. An old army duffel filled with sand was strung from the rafters with a nylon rope cinched through its eyelets. Punching that heavy bag was like punching a bag of cement. You could easily break the architecture of your hand, or fracture one of the thin bones in your foot when landing a roundhouse kick.

A thick piece of lumber nailed to the back wall served as a target board for throwing knives and metal stars. We once placed paper targets on it while testing a home-made .22 caliber zip gun. On late summer nights, wind scorpions and Jerusalem crickets would sometimes cross the floor. Mosquito hawks clung to the walls in solitary audience to the exercises we performed there. A black and white poster of Bruce Lee from *Enter the Dragon* was fixed to the wall. Beside it, a large collage poster of photos documented the seventies life of Hell's Angels. There were snapshots in that poster of snarling German shepherds on taut leashes in the hands of state troopers, long hairs with bandanas and denim vests stitched with the badges of war, photos of badass motorcycles – panheads and shovelheads and choppers with the distinctive rake and trail of their barrel-like forks.

I was mesmerised by one photo in particular.

In this shot, a highway patrolman wearing teardrop aviator glasses stands on the shoulder of a tree-lined road. It looks like a late spring day. Maybe a lake nearby with cottonwood trees shimmering in the light. And he's looking down at the opened pad in his hand as he writes up a ticket – unaware of the Hell's Angel who has snuck up behind him. Stretched tight in the man's fists, the biker holds a thin wire garrote over the officer's unsuspecting head.

In the improvised dojo, we trained hour after hour through summer and winter, fighting the invisible before us. Ridge hands and palm strikes to the temple and to the hollow below the ear. Claw hands to the face. Knife hands to the mastoid and jugular. Hammerfists to the sternum. After finishing a kata – a choreographed series of martial-arts movements – we'd often step out into the cooler air of the backyard. Bare feet in the Bermuda grass. The high-tenor voices of coyotes calling to the dog at Orion's feet.

I was learning how to form a perfect fist. Something about power and movement, how the blade of grass must bend in equal measure to the force of the wind coming through, and how to fall, over and over again, hard, the slap of my hand on the mat below the ringing drum that sent me into the years to come.

34

I pointed to the list and said *Infantry* because I wanted the man in the polyester suit to know, at some unconscious level, that I didn't give a shit what row of ribbons he had pinned to his chest, that I was willing and prepared to crawl through the mud and muck any time of day or night, winter spring summer fall you name it, I was prepared to low-crawl with my face down in the nastiest, foulest, brackish sludge and sewer the world could offer, that I was from Fresno and people from Fresno can take it, can take it in spades and shovelfuls, people from Fresno can take decades of it, that people from Fresno can outcrawl any motherfucker on the planet, or at least crawl with the best of them, low and cold and reptilian. That's why I joined.

35

It's early January, I think. 1981. Dad and I are beyond the eucalyptus trees out front, there in the broken furrows of sand. We're making napalm.

With the San Joaquin Valley's notoriously thick fog to hide our work, we follow a recipe from *The Poor Man's James Bond*. Dad uses the same wood-handled kitchen knife we use to trim fat and meat from vertebrae and gristle for the weekly ham hocks and beans, drawing the flattened edge across a bar of soap to strip thin curling peels into the empty five-gallon paint bucket below.

In another month, I'll be fourteen. Ronald Reagan is in the White House and I'm learning about the Cold War and the Star Wars missile defense shield, the impossible hooks of bra straps and how to build a model volcano out of newspapers and masking tape. I'm also learning that napalm is a gelled substance that can burn right through bone. What I don't know is that my Uncle Jon has seen it put to use. He's smelled what comes after the scorching heat. He's patrolled through jungles and forests I haven't heard of yet. He teaches drama and English classes at Mariposa High School and works the family cattle out on the ranch.

When he visits our house, he gives me books of fiction, poetry, drama. And when he talks about Vietnam, his stories focus on Tudo Street in Saigon, the old French hotel with a dingy courtyard where he stayed, as well as the bars and cathouses where Vietnamese bands played all hours of the night. He says, 'When we landed at Ton Son Nhut air base, we stepped into the fiercest humidity and heat I'd ever encountered. I wanted to vomit. The air was so thick, sluggish, steamy. And smells. I remember the diesel, rotting garbage, excrement, exhaust from thousands of motorcycles, cyclos, trucks, jeeps, and the smell of *nuoc mom*, this Vietnamese food sauce, which I couldn't stand at first. But we got used to it. And fresh breezes would sometimes blow in off the delta, cleared it all out for a short time. Of course, the monsoons would clear the air, too, and then we'd steam as we dried out.'

And Uncle Jon would elaborate like this, circling the thing not talked about: the Combined Military Interrogation Center near the racetrack in Saigon, and places further away:

the cells where he questioned the prisoners in their blue suits, how they huddled in the cages at the zoo, how they begged.

And when one of Dad's friends, the trumpet player Ray Ramos, comes out to teach me how to play the horn, I won't ask him about his time as a mortar man in Vietnam. And Ray won't talk about the burned grass he walked through the morning after the assault when they were nearly overrun by the VC, the smell of the dead drifting over it all, birds singing in the tree line. He won't tell me about the bugle he found beside a Vietnamese soldier who stared at him with his dead eyes. When I come home from my own war, we'll talk about these things. For now, though, he'll tighten his embouchure and place the mouthpiece to his lips, phrasing the twenty-four notes that graveyards know too well.

36

With each can of Coors opened and downed, Dad gets closer and closer to blacking out, closer and closer to resuming his high-altitude reconnaissance missions over Russia's Kamchatka Peninsula, over the year 1965, MIGs rising fast from their airbase to greet him.

Each night he places an oxygen mask over his face and breathes in as the plane lifts off the tarmac of dream, from the airstrip at Eniwetok Atoll or the barren outcrop of Shemya Island in the far north. He checks his gauges. Checks the onboard cameras. Calls out the countdown for the navigator to set his timepiece and mark the stars to chart their way.

Below and above them – the Pacific Ocean and the pale cerulean sky, a vast blue world in its fluid nature, the exosphere stretching out into the drifting reaches of space. He's harnessed into his seat in the well of the fuselage, helmet on, oxygen flowing through the mask, service pistol in its holster, a survival knife in its sheath, while he turns the radio dial away from known Red pilot frequencies, to catch a few moments of Johnny Rivers singing 'Secret Agent Man', a song he's never heard before, even though it seems written solely for him. As the MIGs swing out over the Pacific Ocean in pursuit, Dad listens to Johnny Rivers through the static of his headset.

If the MIGs had shot them down, it would have been reported back home as a training accident.

37

A small group of middle-school boys are filming a Super8 movie – *The War That Time Forgot*. The boys are dressed in green army fatigues and have camouflaged their faces with green and black camo sticks. All of them have fake bloodstains on their uniforms and some have fake blood smeared onto their faces.

Two of these people are the DIRECTOR (my best friend, Brian Voight, aged thirteen) and the main character – SGT T (a thirteen-year-old me). The DIRECTOR places the cast in their positions in the trench while raising his tripod and adjusting the camera, pushing knobs, considering the light level, and looking through the eyepiece to set the framing properly for the shot.

SGT T loads black gunk onto a mascara wand and applies it to the peach fuzz above the lip to simulate a mustache. His air rifle lies where he has placed it – on the dirt mound in front of one of the trenches surrounding the wooden shack fort the soldiers will defend in the next shot. He sits on the far edge of the deep trench and studies his face in a small handheld mirror.

SOLDIER 1 (Ricky, a neighbor and the oldest of the three Goodwin brothers) wipes dirt off the BB gun resting across his legs as he sits at the far end of the trench.

SOLDIER 1

Shawna Allen. Man, oh man. Remember
her in the Christmas play? How'd she get into
those zip-around jeans? She is *so* fine.

DIRECTOR

(To himself . . .)

Who cares how they get in them – it's getting out of them I want to see.

SOLDIER 1

Yeah. I wanna see Shawna Allen unzip those Rag City Blues . . .

SGT T

Should I smoke a cigarette in this shot?

DIRECTOR

You don't have to light it. We can do that on the close-ups. You'd cough anyways.

SOLDIER 1

Do they also make those button-up jeans?

DIRECTOR

I don't know, Ricky. I'm trying to do this . . . Okay, Sgt T, take up your position at the front there.

SGT T

(To SOLDIER 2 – Timmy, aged nine,
who is off to the side with his pants down,

pulling on his penis, oblivious to all else)

Jesus, Ricky, get Timmy to fucking stop –

SOLDIER 1

Hey, you little fucker, get back over here.

DIRECTOR

(Head tilted in surprise)

What're you doing anyways, Timmy?

SOLDIER 2 (Timmy)

If you pull on it, you can make it bigger.

All four SOLDIERS laugh and take up their positions in the foxhole. They point their rifles in the same direction, toward an unseen enemy (OS).

DIRECTOR (CONT'D)

Okay, hold it just like that.

The DIRECTOR depresses the record feature with his left hand and begins ZOOMING IN by turning the main focus knob with his right hand. In the viewfinder, the row of soldiers comes more sharply into view as he shifts the lens to focus on the muzzle – SGT T's rifle barrel.

DIRECTOR (OS)

   And . . . Action!

ENEMY SOLDIERS (the Crandall brothers from down the road) begin jumping into the trench system and fighting SGT T and his SOLDIERS. It is hand-to-hand fighting, in motions slowed deliberately to try to match film speed. We see one rifle buttstock smashed into an ENEMY jaw and the ENEMY dropping slowly, sliding down the sandy wall of the trench and out of sight. Faces twist and contort in pain. The SOLDIERS yell out to one another in the midst of the fighting – their mouths trapped in the silence of 8mm film stock.

   Camera pans to track SGT T as he rises from the trench system and runs with a loaded 12-gauge shotgun through battlefield wreckage and carnage. Smoke drifts across the landscape.

   CLOSE-UP: SGT T'S FACE IN SLOW MOTION AS HE RUNS TOWARD AN ENEMY SOLDIER.

   PULL OUT TO MEDIUM LONG SHOT: WE SEE BOTH SGT T AND THE ENEMY SOLDIER. CUE END MUSIC: SAMUEL BARBER, *ADAGIO FOR STRINGS*.

   SGT T runs up to ENEMY SOLDIER while holding the shotgun in both hands, halts on a dime with the shotgun pointed upward at the ENEMY SOLDIER's face. [Camera note: Take several shots, from various angles (wide, medium and close-up) of both characters. Prop note: Replace ENEMY SOLDIER with armature and 'bearded' watermelon. Melon to be filled with sheep's blood and pig brains from Cherry Auction.]

Final shot. Sgt T pulls the trigger and ENEMY SOLDIER's head explodes in a firework of sheep's blood and pig's brains.

DIRECTOR (CONT'D)
And . . . Cut!

In 1995, in the hospital, they called in the crash cart and had to jump-start my dad with electric paddles. My mother and sister both said that when his eyes rolled back in his head and he slumped over, their field of vision narrowed into a dimly lit tunnel and the noise of the world muted within the curving structure of the ear until they heard nothing at all, or only a low murmur, something like the thrumming of engines. They could see each other's lips mouthing a language that could not be heard. When the nurses and orderlies rushed into the room, they did so in slow motion, as if submerged underwater.

When they describe the moment Dad died, I see the white pills on the blue tray by his bedside rising upward in slow motion, too. The pills ascend one after another the way exhaled air rises in translucent spheres from the dive master's regulator. As Dad's body is touched by figures in blue gowns, red and white carnations drift upward from their glassy vases, their clipped stems a green too bright for the room, glowing in the afternoon light. Slippers, flowers, ballpoint pens, clipboards, small plastic cups, the tray of hospital food separating into sliced rounds of steamed carrots and tiny misshapen globes of split peas – all of it floating in a strange confetti up to the ceiling.

A nurse lifts one of his eyelids slowly with her fingers. She leans over to stare into the closed doorway of a world. What she discovers there sends her running through the chained curtain and into the hallway, waving to someone out of view.

And my father came back to life.

In the recovery room of the ICU, I couldn't help but stare at the strange orange stain of Betadine on his skin where the stitches joined him back together. They'd sawn his sternum wide open to work on his heart, eventually completing a double-bypass and pre-wiring him internally for any possible future heart attacks. Along with the two small wounds on his left leg – where they cut out a section of vein for use in the bypass – he also had a swollen and blackened right eye. The surgeon said it happens sometimes. Patients wake up on the table, confused, scared, in great pain. Like my dad, who must've seen a vision of aliens working over him and came up swinging. That's what the doctor said – Dad had somehow managed to clock the surgeon across the jaw, even after a rotary saw had split his chest open and he was hooked up to all manner of wires and gadgets and tubes. The surgeon hit him back.

He sucked on bits of crushed ice.

His gaze wandered through the framed window and into the tops of the cypress trees beyond, leafed out in a brilliant green. They swayed gently back and forth in the breeze as if an enormous hand were brushing through them with great care.

I leaned over and asked him, 'So what was it like, *dying*?'

'*That*?' he responded, shifting bits of ice to the other side of his mouth so he could speak clearly. 'That was a trauma-junkie's delight.'

When we triggered the device and the napalm exploded, I felt charged and electric. We were surrounded by the cold.

Coffee steamed in the cup as the entire world disappeared in fog. And for a moment, I knew – here was the great body of Death. A portion of the inheritance we all share. I wanted to see it break open in fire. I wanted the world to be shaken by it. And, most of all, I wanted to be shaken by it, too.

40

I said *Infantry* because I didn't really know if I could do it, if I could take it, if it would break me down and chew me up and then continue to keep on chewing. I said *Infantry* because I knew that here was a portion of what work is, here was a portion of what they fed to the lions in the dust and name of Rome. I said *Infantry* because my great-grandfather Carter was gassed during the Battle of Meuse-Argonne in the fall of 1918, the bloodiest battle in American history. He was there in the muck in France during the First World War and yet he still managed to crawl out, through the ruined ground, the world rung into a gear-toothed roar, canisters of gas hissing as they flew over, and he made it back home, though the war would drag him under a few short years later.

I said *Infantry* because one of my great-greats enlisted in the Union Army – 15 November 1861 – at Cumberland Gap, Tennessee, and later served as a corporal in the

Tennessee Volunteers, and even though he'd cracked his back on a green horse at Camp Denison and later contracted rheumatic fever during a bitter December in Knoxville, he stayed on through the fight, from the Confederate horses shot in the river at Shelbyville and on to Huntsville, Alabama, from Bucktown Tavern to Powder Springs to the Siege of Atlanta, from the Battle of Franklin, the Battle of Nashville and the pursuit of General John Bell Hood clear to the Tennessee River.

I raised my hand and said the words *I swear* because I would've been ashamed in the years to come if I hadn't, even if it didn't make sense, even if nobody I cared about ever thought about it, even if all the veterans in my family never said a word, or even if they did, saying, *It's cool, Brian, it doesn't mean a thing, believe me, the uniform doesn't make the man*, or anything along those lines, because it would've meant that between me and the people I revered most there were beaches and jungle foliage and Russian MIGs and snipers and artillery craters and midnights spent drifting on the Pacific under the Southern Cross; between me and the people I most revered there were explosions I couldn't hear, curses and shouting and laughter, engines thrumming, Hueys and Blackhawks lifting from the grass and sand to map the earth in medevac flights that would deliver the wounded to gentle hands in latex gloves, surgeons calling for scalpels and sutures and more blood, type AB negative, while airmen on the flight line hosed bodily fluids from the decks and drank coffee when the day was done.

I said *I, Brian David Turner, do solemnly swear that I will support and defend* because of my grandfather's whiskey-tinged silence as he sat through the Indian Wars of 1970s television, movies euphemistically called Westerns, the sound of Bougainville and Guam and Iwo Jima hovering over him as we lit the Christmas candle and put more wood on the fire.

I signed the paper because I knew that on some deep and immutable level, I would leave and I would never come back.

We moved out from Balad as the winter shifted to spring, and we *talked the guns* to one another on an improvised rifle range on the outskirts of Mosul.

I watched honeybees weighing down the purple heads of flowers with their bright hunger. Behind me, a row of soldiers lying prone in the dirt fired at paper targets duct-taped to boards lined against a sandy berm. Sergeants paced in deliberation behind the firing line, sometimes crouching to advise the riflemen, sometimes pausing to laugh at something just said – their laughter immediately replaced with the reports of M4 carbines and squad automatic weapons. I'd stepped off to the side to relieve myself in the dead grass beyond the firing line, just a short distance from the range, looking back as the other sergeants taught the language of war. Each soldier waiting in turn to exhale the rounds held within. The machine-gunner in each team firing two quick bursts followed by other soldiers in the team shooting in controlled pairs, *pop-pop, pop-pop, pop-pop*. Such patience. Such strange laughter. Such metallic elocution.

Mosul would become our home. We drove through her neighborhoods and walked through her streets. We stopped traffic
and searched vehicles. We scanned the city for heat signatures
in white-hot and black-hot. We drank water and we pissed
and we laughed. We watched porn and listened to Insane
Clown Posse as we drove through the streets, or listened to
Sgt Zapata singing ballads in Spanish that made us think of
California. We kicked in the doors of people's homes and we
put many of them in prison. In Mosul the war became routine.

Each soldier stands in a narrow stall closed off from the world
by a vinyl curtain. In those cramped and private spaces, they
stand under lukewarm streams of water. Some lift their faces
into the thin streams of water with their eyes closed, exhaling
a deep and long-held breath. Others lower their head, as if
under a prayer, to feel the water in its intimate articulation
of the body's surfaces. Of course, most of the soldiers mastur-
bate in the showers, if they're not too exhausted, and even
some of those who are. It's a kind of dream-time spent
standing, whether they'd describe it as such or not. Under

fluorescent lights and falling water, the showers are filled with lovers transported by their own touch. They close their eyes and walk into their apartments and houses back home. Into bedrooms in Michigan and Kentucky, Baltimore and Baton Rouge. And their lovers wait for them. On blue watery sheets made of cotton and silk, their lovers pull back the comforters and welcome them home.

44

Eugene Stoner invented the AR-15, which was modified into the M16 rifle of Vietnam, Somalia, the First and Second Gulf Wars, and Afghanistan. It is the predecessor and cousin of the M4 carbine. The firing pin in the M4 – the pin that strikes the primer and sends the bullet into the world at a muzzle velocity of nearly 3,000 feet per second – is made of chrome-plated carbon steel. It is bright as a smooth-shanked duplex nail. It can easily be held in the palm of your hand.

The upper and lower receivers of the M4, like the one I carried in Iraq, are now forged in places like Graves County, Kentucky. Here is where machinists articulate the lands and grooves of barrel rifling; where the hammer, trigger and sear find their cold housing; where steel is shaped and moulded into a *gas-operated, magazine-fed, selective-fire, shoulder-fired weapon with a telescoping stock*. The steel is made of iron, which comes from ore in the earth's crust; the ore is smelted to remove oxygen while combining the iron with carbon. The last crucial additive element in the making of this particular grade of steel: vanadium. It is a soft, ductile material, bright white in its pure form.

In 1830, the Swedish chemist Nils Gabriel Sefström named vanadium after the Norse goddess Vanadís, whose more familiar name is Freyja. Freyja is the goddess of love and fertility, battle and death. It is Freyja's right to choose from among the slain heroes of battle – dead warriors known as *Einherjar* – so that half of the dead heroes dwell in her great hall in the meadow of Fólkvangar, while the remainder go to Valhalla. When the pad of the index finger, placed against the smooth curve of the trigger, summons the bullet out into the world, it is Freyja we hear in the barrel's report. In the sound of small arms fire, we hear the old drums calling from her great hall in the meadow, that eternal encampment, the army field where dead warriors reside.

Sometimes I imagine Eugene Stoner walking into the great hall at Fólkvangar, holding a smooth and shiny firing pin in his hand. The dead warriors gather around him and repeat the answers he gives to their questions, whispering the words to one another, pondering their weight, saying, *chambering, locking, firing, extracting, ejecting,* over and over. Some of them are puzzled. Confused. Some of them ask, 'These are the principles that have brought us here?'

At one point, I served as a unit armorer with the 10th
Mountain Division out of Ft Drum, near the Canadian border.
I'd sometimes close the massive vault door of the arms' room,
turn off the lights and sit back in a tired vinyl-backed roller
chair as I waited for an old girlfriend to call. I'd remind her
that the room was wired to a remote listening post somewhere
on the base and so I couldn't say anything that wasn't related
to the work of the arms' room. In a darkened room, surrounded
by floor-to-ceiling racks filled with M4s and M16s and M249s
and M240s and M203s and 9mm pistols and Remington
sniper rifles and locked cages packed with night-vision goggles
and much more, I'd listen to the gathering heat of her
breathing, the shuddering of muscle that tremors the breath
and, at its height, cuts it short.

Her voice over the phone, the pace of her breathing – it
spiraled down into that silent, miniature room, the way leaves
tremble on currents of air as they descend, and a tiny man
sat in the darkness below, unable to comprehend the dying
leaves he'd gathered in his arms, the remnants of a distant,
livable world.

The drone pilots sit in their metal connex at the airfield. The connex could be located in Kuwait or Missouri – there's no way to tell from inside. The generator hum blocks out the noise of the outside world. It is a cramped space filled with toggle switches and video-feed monitors, clipboards and laptops.

There are two pilots on shift tonight, with another, their senior, sitting at his desk and researching ice-cream recipes online and now and then commenting to the room when he comes across a recipe he thinks holds promise. One of the pilots switches the onboard camera from black-hot to white-hot and then leans back in his chair. The other pilot doesn't pay any attention to either of them. He stares at the blurry white figures of men gathered beside a house and then realises that they are a flock of sheep penned by the side of some farmer's home. He sighs and slumps, then continues his routine of dropping the yo-yo tied to his middle finger and walking the dog, the only trick he knows.

'Star anise – that's what really makes it work. Damn, that sounds good, doesn't it,' the senior pilot says. 'Damn. It's called Lightly Spiced South African Guava Ice Cream. Some website out of Cape Town.'

The pilot walking the dog says, 'Sounds like you're reading something from *Hustler*.'

'If you think that's sexy, check this shit out. This is how she describes it on the website: "The perfume of fresh guavas drifting through a warm kitchen is one of the quintessential scents of a South African childhood. It's impossible to describe the scent of a perfectly ripe guava to someone who hasn't experienced the coral-pink deliciousness of this most luscious fruit, which you'll find piled high in supermarkets, and on roadside stalls, during South Africa's winter months."'

The men talk mostly through boredom and from the need to stay awake. They are at their loudest when they have a target in sight, the intensity of the room charged in the hunt for souls – but there's a calmness at work then, too: they toggle the zoom lens in smoothly to witness human heat signatures running across a field somewhere in Iraq, one of them stumbling and then pitching over as another pauses to help them stand.

To haunt. This is the drone pilot's charter.

47

A squad of American soldiers sits on the rooftop of an abandoned Iraqi elementary school, most of them spread out and slumped up against the low wall which forms a perimeter around the top of the building. They work in shifts, with a few soldiers pulling watch at key vantage points over the neighborhood below while the others stay low, out of sight, their Kevlar helmets off, one of them using his as a footrest as he lies supine on the coarse surface.

The conversation, for some time now, has focused on masturbation.

– *Let me tell you, men – what you do is make yourself some field pussy.* This is the squad leader. Most of the soldiers laugh. One soldier stares at the star field above, silent, drifting off to some other time. One of them asks – *Field pussy?*

– *Field pussy, yeah. I'm telling you. Finest kind, men. I'm not making this up. See, here's what you do – next time you hit the chow hall, grab an extra banana from that bowl with the apples and fruit and shit.*

Some of the soldiers in the squad tilt their heads toward the sound of his voice, toward his silhouette, which is back-lit in the ambient light of the city at night.

– *And what you do is pocket that banana and leave it back at your hooch for a couple of days.* He spits a copper stream of Copenhagen tobacco in an arc that disappears over the edge of the building, falling into the darkness below. – *You gotta let it get nice and soft and mushy inside, you know? Then, next time you get a chubby, just open the end of that banana and slide right in, smooth as a cheerleader's hot fucking box, men. Slicker'n deer guts on a doorknob, I'm telling ya. Field pussy, men. You haven't lived till you fucked yourself some field pussy.*

The briefing for the night's raid is under way. A five-paragraph operation's order. Officers and sergeants view photographs and aerial footage of the target house, some of them taking notes in small, green pocketbooks, some of them counting the number of houses on the block, some of them drinking coffee, some of them leaning their heads slowly from side to side to crack and release the pressure between vertebrae. While the briefing revolves around trigger men and bomb makers, call signs and radio frequencies, 9-line medevac requests and medical assets, the soldiers outside prepare a terrain model in the hardpan between hooches. Colored lengths of yarn mark phase lines for the raid. Torn pieces of cardboard from an MRE package serve as houses, arranged to resemble a suburban street. And the men laugh and joke with one another while they create the model. They don't talk about the people who live in the target house, third cardboard square from the left. They don't talk about the men eating dinner in that house now, the children who run in through the front door, the sound of their laughter as they turn and run upstairs, their mother calling to them from another room. They just place a small cardboard square on the dirt. A small square that cannot hold the beds they know are inside the house. Dishes in the cupboards. Miniature bottles of

Russian-made medicines stored in the refrigerator door. Photographs from the 1960s and 1970s in frames on wooden tables. Photographs of weddings and lakeside trips and afternoon visits from family members long since dead stored in the bedroom dresser. Nightgowns. Bras. Panties. Sheets folded and neatly stacked.

The soldiers stand around the model – and wait for their sergeants and officers to tell them who it is inside those small brown squares that they might kill tonight, who it is inside the brown squares that might lead them into their last breath. The soldiers stand over the terrain model and peel plastic wrappers from boxes of Marlboro 100s and unfiltered Camels, unhinging their Zippos to burn tobacco and take the smoke of it all into their lungs. Soon they'll have to prep the explosive charges, or 'demo' as they're called, as well as the enemy prisoner of war kits – the EPWs. Team leaders will conduct their final Pre-Combat Inspections. Refilling CamelBaks. Oiling the bolts of their weapons. The drivers will fire up their engines and check their gauges. Across town, a small child kisses her father on his cheek. The soldiers inhale the harsh smoke, lean their heads back and exhale up toward the dead surface of the moon. And – though they darken into silhouettes as the night draws on – the soldiers brighten inside. They crackle in nerve and flame. The gas stations and laundromats and unemployment lines and hardware stores of America disappear. For now, they are soldiers. They are giants standing over the model of someone else's life. Humming with adrenaline, they stand in the great sweep of history – *past, passing, and yet to come* – and take it all in.

49

The soldiers enter the house, the soldiers enter the house.

Soldiers, determined and bored and searing with adrenaline, enter the house with shouting and curses and muzzle flash, det cord and 5.56mm ball ammunition. The soldiers enter the house with pixelated camouflage, flex-cuffs, chem lights, door markings, duct tape. The soldiers enter the house with ghillie suits and Remington sniper rifles, phoenix beacons and night-vision goggles, lasers invisible to the naked eye, rotorblades, Hellfire missiles, bandoliers strapped across their chests. The soldiers enter the house one fire team after another, and they fight brutal, dirty, nasty, the only way to fight. The soldiers enter the house with the flag of their nation sewn onto the sleeves of their uniforms. They enter the house with Toledo and Baton Rouge imprinted on the rubber soles of their desert combat boots. They enter the house and shout 'Honey, I'm home!' and 'Heeeeeeere's Johnny!' The soldiers enter the house with conversations of *Monday Night Football* and the bouncing tits of the Dallas

Cowboys' cheerleaders. The soldiers enter the house with cunt and cooch, cock wallet and butcher's bin on their tongues. The soldiers enter the house with paperbacks in their cargo pockets, *Starship Troopers* and *Black Hawk Down*, *We Were Soldiers Once and Young*. The soldiers enter the house *Straight Outta Compton* or with Eminem saying, 'Look, if you had one shot, or one opportunity'. They enter the house with their left foot, they enter the house the way one enters cemeteries or unclean places. The soldiers enter the house with their insurance policies filled out, signed, beneficiaries named, last will and testaments sealed in manila envelopes half a world away. The soldiers enter the house having just ordered a new set of chrome mufflers on eBay for the Mustang stored under blankets in a garage north of San Francisco. The soldiers enter the house with only nine credits earned toward an associate's degree in history from the University of Maryland. They kick in the door and enter the house with the memory of backyard barbecues on their minds. They kick in the door while cradling their little sisters in their arms. They kick in the door and pull in the toboggans and canoes from the hillsides and lakes of Minnesota. They kick in the door and bring in the horses from the barn, hitching them to the kitchen table inside. The soldiers enter the house with Mrs Ingram from the 2nd grade at Vinland Elementary School. The soldiers enter the house with Mrs Garoupa from Senior English at

Madera High. The soldiers kick in the door and enter the house with their arms filled with all the homework they ever did. They enter the house and sit down to consider the quadratic equation, the Socratic Method. The soldiers enter the house to sit cross-legged on the floor as the family inside watches on, watches how the soldiers interrogate them, saying, *How do I say the word for 'friend' in Arabic? How do I say the word 'love'? How do I tell you that Pvt Miller is dead, that Pvt Miller has holes in the top of his head? And what is the word for ghosts in Arabic? And how many live here? And are the ghosts Baath Party supporters? Are the ghosts in favor of the coalition forces? Are the ghosts here with us now? Can you tell us where the ghosts are hiding? And where the ghosts keep their weapons cache and where they sleep at night? And what can you tell us about Ali Baba? Is Ali Baba in the neighborhood?* The soldiers enter the house and take off their dusty combat boots and pull out an anthology of poetry from an assault pack, *Iraqi Poetry Today*, and commence reading poems aloud. The soldiers say, 'This is war then: All is well.' They say, 'The missiles bomb the cities, and the airplanes bid the clouds farewell.' The soldiers remove their flak vests and turn off their radios. The soldiers smile and stretch their arms, one of them yawning, another asking for a second cup of chai. The soldiers give chocolates to the frightened little children in the shadows of the house. The soldiers give chocolates to the frightened little children and teach them how to say *fuck you* and how to flip off the world. The soldiers recite poetry as trays of chai and tea and cigarettes are brought into the room. The soldiers, there in the candlelight of the front room, with the Iraqi men of military age zip-tied with flex-cuffs, kneeling, sandbags over their heads, read verses from *Iraqi Poetry Today*. The soldiers switch off their night-vision goggles and set their padded helmets on the floor while the frightened little children pretend to eat the chocolate they've been given, their mothers shushing them when they begin to cry. And the soldiers, men from Kansas and California, Tacoma and College Station – these soldiers remove the black gloves from their hands to show the frightened little children how they mean no harm, how American the soldiers are, how they might bring in a pitcher of water for the bound and blinded men to drink from soon, perhaps, if there's time, and how they read poetry for them, their own poetry, in English, saying, 'Between time and time, between blood and blood. All is well.' *All is well*, the soldiers say. The soldiers kick in the doors and enter the house and zip-tie the men of military age and shush the women and the frightened little children and drink the spooned sugar stirred into the hot chai and remove their stinking boots and take off their flak vests and stack their weapons and turn off their night-vision goggles and say to the frightened little children, softly, with their palms held out in the most tender of gestures they can offer, their eyes as brown as the hills that lead to the mountains, or as blue as the rivers that lead to the sea – *'All is well, little ones, all is well.'*

50

Dirty, exhausted, silent – the platoon sits on the far side of the chow hall, eating breakfast from Styrofoam plates. A thin stream of milk ropes and swirls into the coffee as I pour and mix it with a spoon.

On the big screen television set against the far wall, Armed Forces Network News pipes in programs like CNN and *Good Morning America.*

In America, a pet owner shuts a glass and metal door before turning on the machine. A chocolate-colored French poodle stares through the glass with its large brown eyes. Foamy suds and water coat the insides of the machine as the reporter laughs and asks the pet owner about the dog's state of mind, how quickly the dog has taken to this type of cleaning.

I continue to eat my breakfast, in the desert of a foreign country, while back home jets of air lift the dog's fur and scatter tiny droplets of water.

A shipping container reverberated with music beside the prisoner containment areas – *the kennels,* as some called them. Bruzik and I would sometimes look over at the container before continuing on to our vehicle. There was a sign painted over the connex labeling it The Discotheque. I remember saying, 'Fucking pogues even hang out in their own god-damned club.'* I thought the pogues were drinking chai and kicking back listening to music in their self-styled chill spot. What I didn't realise: I was listening to the inter-rogator's craft. Inside those metal boxes, men were being broken down and changed for ever. Music blared at them, lights strobed sleep-deprived minds. Stress positions: think through the answers, think through the questions. Or say nothing at all. Later, I heard the dogs barking in those strange chambers, but I never saw the prisoners kneeling outside in the rain. I never fully appreciated the depth of the cold a night in Mosul could offer a man's body, the hypothermic value of intelligence. Or the need for sanitary gloves, a rectal thermometer.

I sometimes tried to imagine Ft Huachuca, Arizona. Instructors writing key passages from the Geneva Convention with brittle chalk sticks on a classroom blackboard. The

---

* Pogues – soldiers not actively engaged in combat.

definition of 'Interrogation and the Intelligence Cycle' detailed in *Field Manual 34-52: Human Intelligence Collector Operations*. The history of interrogation outlined for the students, chapter by chapter, in the desert heat fifteen miles from the border with Mexico – along with terms like *environmental deprivation* and *fear up harsh, emotional love approach* and *emotional hate approach*.

At some point, though I'm not sure when exactly, I quit thinking about Ft Huachuca. But Ft Huachuca never stopped thinking about me.

52

The drone aircraft flies from north to south and back again, in slightly overlapping passes, as it works its steady way over the rooftops of Baghdad. The camera clicks in its housing when the drone pilot recognises the target neighborhood from a list of surveillance priorities.

At night, photographic mapping is a matter of heat and cold. By day, as in sculpture, it is a matter of shadows articulated by light.

The bomb maker is a careful and patient man, working his trade on a long wooden bench. Wiping the sweat from his forehead, from the back of his neck, with a handkerchief. Drying the palms of his hands before resuming his trade. A pair of thin bulbs hang over the work surface from metal hooks screwed into the ceiling plaster. In the background, a surprising music plays on a portable CD player, 'Crystal Blue Persuasion', by Tommy James and the Shondells, though maybe it's some other song from some other time. And the bomb maker hums under his breath as he arranges the materials along the length of the bench.

There may be children in the house, somewhere upstairs or in one of the other rooms on the main floor, but there's no way of telling from inside this room. If we were to subtract the sounds around him now, subtract the Blackhawks on patrol over the city somewhere in the distance, subtract the occasional car grinding a gear or applying the calipers of worn brake pads at a nearby vehicle checkpoint run by the Iraqi National Guard, if we could erase the whirring sound of the neighborhood generator shack and the image of its attendant in silhouette, his grease-coated hands as dark as his shadow; and if we could erase the low drone and fizz of the light bulbs illuminating the product of his labor, subtract the music on the CD player, subtract the scuffing sound the soles of his sandals make when he shifts his weight and moves the explosives to another part of the bench, subtract the second hand ticking its way toward zero on his wrist, then, underneath it all, we might hear the steady ebb and flow of the bomb maker's breathing. Deep within the man's brain, down inside the medial temporal lobe, the amygdala seems to have shut off, as if the bomb maker's emotional center has been hushed into listening as well. At the level of the basal brain, the bomb maker's medulla oblongata continues to regulate the autonomic systems of his body so that his eyes might focus with all their clarity on that which lies before him under two cones of diffused light.

The hollow shell of an old rusted-out 155mm artillery round sits on the bench to his left. Several spools of wire rest on a pegboard, along with a clipboard of photocopied instructions, wire cutters and snips, a roll of duct tape. The bomb maker takes down the tools he needs and considers where this bomb might be placed. Perhaps hidden among the piles of discarded trash under a highway overpass, where the blast can randomly maim by means of the acoustic nature of the archway even if the shell fragments can't wound or kill their intended victims. It might be given a remote detonating system, like a rigged cell phone, or a camouflaged wire unspooled to a position far enough away from the diameter of the blast. It may be in the trunk of an abandoned car, in the belly of a dead farm animal, lie buried in the roadbed or built into a brick wall down a narrow lane.

This is the kind of bomb that – if set in the right location and detonated at just the right moment – might make the evening news in America or in the UK. This is the bomb that kills twenty-seven in a marketplace on a Tuesday afternoon and injures forty more. It can devastate a traffic circle, or a police station with its officers lined up waiting for their pay. It can kill in the city just as much as it can kill on a two-lane country road in the farmlands north of Baghdad. The hospitals and morgues know this bomb's potential. If an Iraqi doctor were to stand beside the bomb maker and consider the object before him, he would see gurneys wheeled in from Red Crescent ambulances. Voices calling through tiled corridors. Mothers wailing. Relatives, fists balled, gritting their teeth. Children in the hospital beds staring into the fluorescent tubes of light above, dying, coughing up the blood in their lungs. A janitor guiding a mop head over the trail leading to the emergency room.

Still. How amazing it is to breathe. For the fist-sized pump of the heart to signal the body's internal clock, minute by minute, for a lifetime. The simple fact that this bomb maker can work on a bomb without realising he's humming along with Tommy James's chorus, it's something that slips between the surfaces of this world. Singing. A quiet, nearly inaudible chant, it's true. But singing all the same. That birdlike quality.

The moment requiring, even if only in the smallest degree, a layer of beauty to be transposed over the assembly of Death's cold and metallic invitation. Singing.

And when he makes the one mistake which the explosives cannot condone, in one smooth motion he is lifted in a wave of shock and shearing fragments that separate arms and legs from the trunk of his body. There is an absence of singing, a complete absence of the human voice. There is only the dust and the swirling sound of the explosion pressing the cerebellum and the hippocampus down onto the stem of his brain, shock wave after shock wave. And in the bomb maker's ruined face there may be a momentary recognition of the gaping hole where the explosive force of the blast ripped open the back wall of his home – where the bomb maker thinks he can see the angels written of in 'The Exordium' of the Qu'ran, the passage in which the angels appointed to guard the hole that serves as the gateway to hell tend to those souls hoping to escape.

The bomber is dead, it's true, but others are waiting.

54

In one of the shower trailer stalls on Forward Operating Base (FOB) Marez, Esposito stands under a showerhead and thinks of his home town, his neighborhood, his house. He turns a

gritty disc of soap in his hands and watches its bright trans-
formation into foam and air. After another deep exhalation of
breath, Esposito simply leans forward to press his forehead
against the stall's blue plastic molding. He is leaning his forehead against the abiding structure of the world, pressing the
neocortex and the frontal lobe against its inscrutable nature.
When he opens his eyes, he's in the cab of his old pickup with
his wife Sherry sitting on the bench seat beside him. Audioslave
sings 'Like a Stone' on the radio. And he can feel the cool
strands of Sherry's dark hair when he draws his fingers through
and gently lets them fall slack to their ends. The truck, its
gearshift in neutral, rolls through the automatic car wash in
a blur of soap and giant sponge brushes spinning blue. Esposito
almost laughs out loud when Sherry turns to bite the fleshy
lobe of his right ear, just enough for the nerves to twinge and
spark, before saying to him, 'That's how you know I love you,
honey – I'm the only one who knows all the little painful things
that give you pleasure.'

55

Our platoon functions as the Quick Reaction Force out of FOB
Patriot on some days, a base located on the shoreline of the
Tigris River in the heart of Mosul.

I have misgivings, mostly because the base is targeted

consistently by a 122mm mortar crew, but it also has a dusty little cantina where soldiers can drink chai or soda and watch music videos of Arabic and Turkish pop stars. Most soldiers smoke cigarettes and stare at the belly dancers and foreign rappers on television. Outside, it's possible to catch a glimpse of SSG Kaha, a mere figure in silhouette on a nearby rooftop, frozen in a classic t'ai chi stance. There is also a female Iraqi interpreter with dark red hair, hair dyed the color of blood in the movies, who wears a double pistol belt with a 9mm handgun on each hip – which is one of the reasons we all call her Two Guns. And there is a scrawny fourteen-year-old Iraqi boy who apparently, because his English is incredible and because he is a lion in a child's body, lives on the base. He yells at the middle-aged Iraqi laborers in an admixture of Arabic and English, exhorting them to move faster 'you dirt-bags, faster god-dammit, listen to me or I will fire your lazy ass and get some other douche-bag to work for me'. The men keep their heads down as they transport each pallet of bricks or stack sandbags up against the building façades or dip their hands wrist deep into a slurry of cement to test the consistency of it.

56

Pvt Miller wrote a short message while sitting in a port-o-let in the motor pool on FOB Patriot.

Pvt Miller placed his squad automatic weapon on its buttstock, leaned over to take the muzzle of the barrel into his mouth. A mongoose paused under an orange tree down by the river. And then Pvt Miller depressed the trigger to put about six rounds through the top of his skull.

57

I didn't hear the sound of the weapon when it fired. I'd just eaten breakfast in a green canvas tent with folding tables and chairs. There were boxes of cereal arranged in rows on one of the tables, cartons of whole milk half submerged in a slush of ice. I grabbed a can of Coke and was walking up the hill with the river to my back when our squad radios instantly filled with chatter and cross talk, all static pops and urgent voices and electricity. And even though I didn't have a clue what had just happened, I knew somebody was hurt, that one of us was hurt, maybe more, and I ran back down the hill to descend into it.

58

That night, I helped the platoon sergeant and Bruzik go through Pvt Miller's duffel bag, rucksack and assault pack in his hooch. We were tasked with dividing up Miller's personal effects from any military equipment the army required as part of its inventory. By tradition, as I understood it, his weapon should be destroyed. We folded his army combat uniforms (or ACUs) and placed them with his winter combat boots in the duffel headed home. Walkman, headphones, a small stack of compact discs – all went in the duffel with his name, unit and the last four digits of his social security number stenciled on its side with black spray paint. We stood in the dim fluorescent light of that room and scanned through his magazines and personal effects because the platoon sergeant said we wanted to make sure that we didn't send anything home that might disturb his mother.

Our platoon leader was one of the finest officers I served with during my years of service. As I lay in my own rack that night and thought about all that had happened that day, I realised he must be trying to formulate the words and sentences to an impossible letter home, words meant to convey our own loss within the platoon and to console a family continents away. And I saw the duffel bag I had helped to pack as it was delivered to their front doorstep. The sound of the doorbell ringing inside, too shrill, I think, too bright. Wintertime still, there on the East Coast, the men on the porch wearing long black coats. A neighbor pushing a baby stroller down the sidewalk and pausing to adjust her wool scarf before telling the men, her voice hesitating some, that they should knock on the side door near the back. The two men thanking her before one of them hoists the weight of the duffel onto his shoulder and follows the other man to where the tears will come.

As far as I could tell, the weapon wasn't destroyed. It was turned in to the unit armorer, cleaned up, and quietly kept in the arms room for the next rotation.

59

The war is almost over in the Pacific. Under his helmet – the samurai's headband. A white scarf worn loosely around his neck. He also has a silk band, called a *sennin-bari*, with the hair of one thousand women sewn into it. There should be high-school girls on the flight line, too, he thinks, as he'd heard it's done in Kyushu, smiling and singing and waving sprigs of cherry blossoms when the pilots pass by. But here, so far from home, there is only the fluttering of a flag overhead, a salt breeze: all that the day has designated for ruin.

Early this morning, he drank mizu with his fellow kamikaze, singing an ancient song before stepping into the last day of a life. Unlike some of the other pilots, he is actually of samurai descent, and so he folded strands of his hair into a rough envelope of paper as a last memento for his family.

Before leaving the briefing room, he asked that it be sent to them along with a letter and a final poem for his wife, as well as the will he penned last night.

The flight crews attend to their Zeroes as he walks in slow motion toward them. They remove chock blocks from the wheels and recheck the engine cowling to confirm the ammunition is seated properly. Some of them glance up now and then as the pilots near, their eyes quick and dark and curious. He takes no notice of them – his gaze remaining focused on the single pale cherry blossom painted on his fighter. His tongue feels coarse and swollen from last night's sake, with a slight noxious fume of vomit lingering at the back of his throat. Curses and singing linger there, too. Along with all that he wanted to say when he staggered out and pissed into the direction he thought Tokyo lay, before the night's stoic landscape hushed him into lying back on the cool grass and left him spinning hard into the liquor's dive. A field of stars too soon erased by the morning light. By now, the broken bottles and smashed chairs from the farewell hall have been cleared away, the debris swept up and carted off to the burn pile at the base perimeter.

Across the wide sweep of the morning's light, HMS *Formidable* plies the ocean, its anti-aircraft crews oiling their weapons in readiness for the likes of him and speaking to each other in the language of Dickens and Wilde, authors he'd enjoyed at university. And it seems to him that a meaningful quote should rise to the occasion and guide him through the ineluctable steps leading to fire and silence, but instead each mundane feature of the world calls attention to itself – dials and numbers and gauges, the goggles fitted to his face, the feel of his tongue on the surface of his chapped lips, controls for rudder and flaps, the vertical stabiliser, even the translucent surface of the cockpit glass which flattens the sunlight into a dull glare.

60

Sixty years later, in 2004, could the young Iraqi woman preparing herself in the far room of the house feel as that kamikaze felt the day he walked toward his plane, before his morning shifted into a pitched dive from blue to blue, his life driven into the metal-clad surface of the ship's flight deck, his body transformed from water to fire to smoke?

She stares a moment into a handheld mirror. Perhaps she does this because there is a deep and abiding human need to fully recognise all that the world will soon lose. A kind of inward grieving, maybe, even as the voices in the next room call out to her to don the vest they have worked through the night to create, even as the languid old cat stretches on the floor beside her feet, a droplet of water swelling on the under-side of the faucet's lip.

And when she leans in close to study the water, another version of herself bends its shadowy form in the fluid's convex lens, her legs disappearing beneath her, arms spreading outward, as if practicing the motion, her fingertips and palms already deep within the vanishing to come.

61

My team swung wide around the fallen blast walls. The explosion had blown several of the giant concrete barriers from their protective line around the police station, huge letter 'Ts' scattered in the boulevard. There was a hole in the roadbed large enough to fit a mid-sized car.

Our job was a simple one: set up a security perimeter on the far side of the scene so that others could deal with the trauma and the debris. This is where sixteen Iraqi policemen stood on the sidewalk in one moment, vanished in the next. A forearm still attached to a hand, a wedding band shining on a finger. Dust. A strange and momentary silence. Where do you place the small numbered flags? There is a mustache, alone, on a sidewalk.

In a small town south-east of the city, I watched a crew of boys scavenge the bombed-out shells of their former lives. Each morning, they would cross the dirt fields, hoist themselves up onto the swaying rooftops, and then sledge the plaster and brick until they could get at the steel rebar. They were salvaging scrap. Hour after hour they took turns with the sledgehammer. The rhythmic report of the hammer face resounded off the structures. They stood on the crown of that dead god, slamming bone, insistent that the skull's hemispheres break open so they might climb down inside the strange creature. Sometimes they'd pause to hoist a jug of water to their lips, a long pull to slake their thirst. And when the sun rose to its apex and the heat became unbearable with its own implacable fist, the boys hoisted themselves down inside, disappearing into the shadows.

And they did the impossible. They hammered at one of those buildings until the plaster and brickwork crumbled free in shards falling to the ground below. They exposed the metal framework within. The building stared at me across the dirt fields with its open-framed eyes, smoking with plaster and dust drifting out, as I stood guard at the firebase and listened to the boys laughing from somewhere inside that dead king's skull.

Mosul is inside me. All of its buildings. All of its smoke and pollution. Its 1.7 million people. The university district and the bridges over the winding river. Barber shops and ice trucks and sheep grazing in the ruins of Nineveh. Minarets. Water buffalo in the eucalyptus groves where the rotting uniforms of Saddam's military continue to disappear. The dead Canadians out by the television station. The Kurdish pesh-merga standing guard behind sand-bagged machine-gun emplacements stationed around their regional political office. Old men staring from the automotive shops. The birdlike bodies of their grandchildren chasing after us through the neighborhoods. The ghosts rising from the mist along the river. The slow-moving ghosts in the streets and alleys of Mosul. The many ghosts returning to their homes each night to sleep with the ones they love.

Dead tanks rust in a graveyard of metal beyond the outskirts of the city, like skeletons in a field. They remind me of images of German and French and British soldiers left on the battlefields of the First World War. Their jawbones unhinged. Small tufts of hair clinging to the curvature of the skull, the way saw grass clings to the dunes by the sea. Wind blowing through them, as through a flute.

A short walk from Nagasaki train station and beyond a retail outlet hawking black t-shirts emblazoned with *I am not American* lies the Daikoku Golf and Batting Center, located on the rooftop of a multi-level car park. It's late June 2012, eight years since I left Iraq and nearly seventy years since my grandfather fought as a Marine in the Pacific. And there's no need for an official thermometer reading – it's so humid out I can taste it. The air is tinged with ship diesel, motorcycle exhaust, Chinese noodle shops searing grease into cast-iron woks. I can feel the heat stress in the soaked jersey clinging to my body. I pause to take in the high green netting and the rooftop antennas on the nearby buildings, the afternoon given a heavy stillness, as if the world were listening to my breathing, amplified by the foam-padded batting helmet I'm wearing.

The lightbox assembly switches from red to green as the metal arm of the pitching machine, coiling back on its springs, rocks forward to deliver a 70-mph two-seamed fast-ball, high and rising. The hard thud of the ball thwacks against the loosely hanging vinyl backdrop as I swing through the pitch and finish with a mumbled curse toward the gods of baseball.

I've come here to clear my head, to tell myself that the world is still only the world. I want to do something other than contemplate the widening circle of war, the bomb, the *hibakusha* who fled Hiroshima only to be bombed a second time here in Nagasaki.

Baseball. Pitching machines humming the way cicadas sing in the noontime trees of the nearby park. Curveballs and knuckleballs and the sixty feet and six inches between release and contact. The merits of all that is possible and all that is probable weighed within the motion of that flight.

And there's no escaping it. 11.02 a.m. The 'Fat Man' falling. The bells ringing. An official with the Nagasaki Prefectural Office has sent a team of individuals out into the streets. It is their task to count the dead, the dead who worked their way to any cool water they could find. They count them as they float. They count them as the tide carries them out to sea.

When my upper body turns on the next pitch, a slider that discovers the sweet spot in my swing, the barrel of the bat launches the ball into the blue ether – it rises and keeps rising, it is a small spinning sphere made to hover where only I can see it, an aerial sculpture ascending to where the bomb burst into light and screaming wind, the hypocenter below a hallowed space I will walk in tomorrow, at 11.02 a.m., when the bells ring and the dead cry out in their broken voices, those who cannot find what they search for, blinded in the flash, calling out for water – they always call for water.

A Marine infantryman, my grandfather – Papa – landed in the first wave on the beaches of Guam. July the 21st 1944. He'd already survived Bougainville. The black sands of Iwo Jima would come later. Then the pamphlets teaching rudimentary Japanese, the preparation for the invasion of Japan – plans superseded by the Bomb.

This is the narrative I've carried with me all my adult life. A few sentences strung together in the brief sketch of a life at war. The order of battle. The lifeline of a war. My grandfather's war.

I wonder what it must have been like for him, a farm boy from rural Arkansas. He moved to San Francisco not long before the war, and after joining the Marine Corps and training at Camp Elliott in San Diego, he took a troopship across the Pacific to New Zealand, where the 3rd Marines initially trained. He must have seen the Hauraki Gulf at Auckland and the Bay of Plenty, or sailed further south to the Cook Strait at Wellington.

He must have heard about the sailors who drowned one night during a failed landing exercise in rough seas, near

Paekakariki, and thought of the many ways that he might die, too. By bayonet or kamikaze. Drowning. Malaria. By submarine, field howitzer, heavy machine gun. The list ongoing. And I wonder if he saw the First Lady, Eleanor Roosevelt, when she visited the troops in September that year and, in tan cap and skirt suit, leaned forward to rub noses with a Maori woman in traditional dress.

Did he explore the streets of Wellington with his buddies, visiting milk bars and wandering into the Taranaki area, perhaps to pass by the two-story house painted red at 318 Upper Willis Street? Did he smile when the MPs stationed at the front gate tried to stare the men down, one of them saying, 'Scoot on, boys. The merchandise in this place is too hot for you to handle. I can promise you that.'

67

My great-uncle Johnny still went to the movies in San Francisco while Papa was serving. Popcorn and a drink in hand, Great-uncle Johnny sat in the darkened theater and watched as the newsreels of the day began to play. The announcer calling out the action, delineating the distant narrative as an amphibious assault takes place south of where the sun sets each day. Marine assault vehicles began their island approach. Their rear troop ramp was a Japanese invention.

And then – something that must have instantly pushed uncle Johnny to the edge of his seat: the image of his brother in a landing craft approaching the beaches of Guam. He was certain that he'd seen him – so certain that he immediately left the theater in order to bring his mother back for the next showing.

He should have stayed to watch the newsreel to the end. A few frames later Papa's landing craft took a direct hit and the newsreel cut to another image, some other moment in the war.

The explosion ripped the landing craft apart and Papa was thrown into the water. He did his best to stay under and swim his way to the beachhead, surfacing as little as possible. I sometimes imagine him underwater there, the strange and horrific world sounding itself above and reverberating down, the naval gunfire, the explosions, the screaming engines of men in their winding-down pain. Could he see the seafloor below or the contrails of bullets angling through the water around him? I sometimes imagine him sinking to the bottom, his rifle slipping through his fingers, his helmet drifting in the current above him with a slow-motion tip and roll as it empties of light and fills with shadow. If I listen hard enough I can hear a 250-horsepower Continental landing craft coughing and chugging at full throttle when the boatmaster shifts gears for the assault, the heavy barrels of the .50-caliber machine guns smoking as blasts of sea spray rise above the Continental and rain down on the men inside, the men who hunch over and vomit on their own boots, and I can see the inch or so of water inside the deck of the craft sloshing with portions of their half-digested breakfast of steak and eggs, floating forward and back with the lurch and dip of the tide, the boom of the surf getting closer, fighter planes in close air support, dropping bombs that wobble and tumble in the air, erupting on the ridgelines beyond the beach.

Who wouldn't walk the ocean floor, given the world of men above? Who wouldn't turn and walk the other way – down into the vast abyss of the ocean, down into the watery dark, where the creatures of the deep must gather to witness what the cerebellum is capable of?

It is now family folklore – the story of how Great-uncle Johnny saw Papa that day. But I've never considered the camera placement inside the story; I've never considered the cameraman in the landing craft. Papa tells me that he had been certain all had perished in the blast, his entire platoon, until years after the war, when he bumped into another survivor on the street – again in San Francisco. But what happened to the cameraman? Probably killed, and the driver of the craft turned the footage in once he was back shipside.

I never considered the cameraman because I have become the camera – its images preserved through the words with which Papa and my parents created the story, the words I've shifted and reshifted, viewing the scene over and over as the years go by. When it comes down to it, we are the camera. The cameraman – even the living one on that landing craft – lives outside the historical moment. But I'm now there, I'm there with Papa's younger self, seasick and scared shitless.

68

Aunt Karen tracked down the original newsreel, and had a still photograph made from the grainy film stock of that day. I have a copy of this photograph at home, with Papa in a shadowy mist staring grim-faced and determined at all that I cannot see when I hold it in my hands. Great-uncle Johnny and Nana waited months to hear – via a yellow faded Marine Corps letterhead note – that he'd survived, that he'd made it.

69

Papa sits in his chair, hour after hour, as Saturday afternoon war movies and westerns drone on the television. I am four years old. Mom helps me assemble an ornate felt owl from a craft kit and a bottle of Elmer's glue on the coffee table while Grandma Anna dollops a tablespoon of mayonnaise into a bowl of tuna fish and sliced pickles. Papa sits in his recliner the way he once slumped against a sand berm on the beachhead on Guam, trying to catch his breath, a Browning automatic rifle resting across his legs, his hands shaking with alcohol.

70

Yukio Muramatsu pitched for Nagoya – the baseball team now known as the Chunichi Dragons – before being drafted into the Imperial Army. He served in China and then deployed to Guam. The US Navy raised its guns and began the bombardment of the island on 8 July 1944. Three days later, airplanes began dropping bombs, and the shelling continued until the 21st. While the navy battered Guam, my grandfather and the 3rd Marines waited on the tiny atoll at Eniwetok and prepared for the attack.

A Japanese star. And, in less than a week, Yukio would be dead.

I stood in my parents' kitchen as Papa hoisted his left leg up to rest his foot on the seat of a dining-room chair. 'I don't think I've ever shown anyone this – except my wife, of course,' he said, rolling his pant leg up to reveal a wide, pink, horizontal scar, maybe three inches long, at the midway point of his shin. 'I got this on Guam.'

Other than Grandma, he hadn't shared this with anyone – for over sixty-five years.

The 3rd Marines were tasked with holding the extreme left flank of the division on the western side of the island. Today, a Harley-Davidson dealership sits just off what's now called Marine Corps Drive – where the bulk of the invasion troops landed that day. Just up the road, the Governor's office and a museum sit in a grove of trees. My grandfather and his fellow Marines had to fight their way up the Chonito cliffs as Japanese soldiers from the 320th Independent Infantry Battalion lobbed grenades and mortars. Sixty years later a Japanese Ha-go tank would sit beyond the beachhead in salt-rusted decrepitude with a ten-foot-tall emaciated-looking Godzilla replica calling out in a frozen, silent language over the scene.

Dad wrote me in an email:

There were no sandy beaches for Papa. Just the cliffs. When they finally got to the top, his unit took cover in a cemetery. It was dark; they were exhausted and hungry and scared and they were attacked and the damn Japanese just wouldn't drop when they were shot. And shot again and again. At dawn it was evident that the Marines had definitely 'killed' every tombstone in the cemetery – along with 400 plus actual Japanese soldiers. Papa only laughed about the headstones.

Papa never spoke to me of that long night on Guam, or the nights to follow. He was a man of historical silence. It wasn't until I was ready to ship out to Iraq that he spoke directly to me of anything that had to do with combat. In the family living room, he cautioned me to pick up the biggest weapon I could get when shit hit the fan. *Carry all the ammo you can,* he told me. *You'll be glad you did when the time comes.*

72

When I was a boy, we'd play catch out on the street in front of his house, the rough surface of the road separating us. We'd talk about baseball and how he'd played before the outbreak

of the war, stories of Satchel Paige and Joe DiMaggio and
Lefty Grove, the old leather glove on his hand the same he'd
used as a utility infielder.

There's a meditative quality to playing catch. It makes me
wonder if he sometimes drifted off to the headstones. The bullets.
The men. A world of sound I can't imagine ever dying out.

73

I'm staying at the Savoy Hotel in Berlin. It's autumn 2011. I'm
at a sidewalk table outside the Vienna Bar, staring at lovers
strolling down the boulevard and waiting for my meal. From
the menu, I've ordered:

Austrian Mountain Cheese Soup 5,50 €
Fried Black Pudding with Potatoes and Cabbage 13,50 €
Viennese Apple Strudel 6,50 €

The waitress, who could be the great-granddaughter of
the man who loaded a canister of gas into the artillery piece
that would take nearly fourteen years to kill my own great-
grandfather Harley, returns to my table to pour me a glass of
red wine, waiting with a smile for my approval of its bouquet.

And I can see the Germans in the cities and villages Harley
had never heard of and maybe never would. The Germans kiss

their loved ones goodbye in Augsburg and Bremen. The young men board the trains and little children race after them as the belching steam forms clouds which soon vanish before them. Milk cows graze in a pasture not far from the Baltic Sea, where a mother and father sit in the front room in silence, a small fire in the hearth, their son gone. The son who will pivot to slide the canister into the artillery piece that will be launched into the air above the Battle of Meuse-Argonne. It will take my great-grandfather until 1932 to die, the delay of his death making my own life possible. I do not know the German's name, but I can stand by the window in the front room with his mother and father. I can watch the cows outside, the shift of light crossing the field as the day completes itself. Listen to his father describe the loss of an uncle at the Battle of Mars-La-Tour in 1870, known in the family as a valiant cavalryman who charged the French guns with the Prussian 7th, saber in hand. And I can listen to his mother say, *'Wird eine Familie ausgeloescht.'**

74

Iwo Jima, Pacific Ocean. 1945.

The 3rd Marines are already ashore. Several waves have landed. The initial hush has turned to blood and horror, muzzles and cannons. Bullets. Shelling. Spigot mortars and

---

* 'This is how a family is extinguished.'

mines. Marines crawling in volcanic ash. On Mt Surabachi, hidden doors open briefly for Japanese artillery to fire their rounds before sealing them safely shut within the tunneled mountain.

At some point much later in the course of the fight for the island, my grandfather will carry two tanks with a harness strapped to his back. He will guide Japanese men from their holes in the earth with a mixture of fuel and compressed gas, men who scream in agony as he lifts their scorched voices into ash with a flamethrower's stream of fire.

75

There is something in the landscape itself that makes me circle back to it, whether it's jungle or the American West, the woodlands of France, the American South, deserts, rivers, beaches – all perceived, in some ways, as wild spaces, where the architecture of civilisation is not at play, the context of human society somehow absent or suspended. A space where the rules are upended. The theater of war, some call it. The space where war disentangles itself from the structure of human norms to thrash into the natural world, the idea of beauty, all that some might view as the closest this world can come to a kind of sacred perfection.

This is part of the intoxication, part of the pathology of it all. This is part of what I was learning, from early childhood on – that to journey into the wild spaces where profound questions are given a violent and inexorable response, that to travail through fire and return again – these are the experiences which determine the making of a man. To be a man, I would need to walk into the thunder and hail of a world stripped of its reason, just as others in my family had done before me. And, if I were strong enough, and capable enough, and god-damned lucky enough, I might one day return clothed in an unshakeable silence. Back to the world, as they say.

76

Who can say what made Papa raise his left arm on a December morning in the Solomon Islands? What was it that caught his attention? The Marine patrol stopped, each man crouching down the way ferns curl their fronds inward to the touch. The root-buttressed boles of whitewood trees rose high above them, their green canopies filtering shafts of light, holding it in clusters near the topmost branches. Island lychee rose ninety feet high in a burst of red-hued leaves. One of the Marines considered the ripening fruit hanging overhead, thin-skinned with a blackening peel, and for a brief moment he thought the tree appeared to branch into leaves of flame.

High up in the canopy, a lone skink ate from an epiphyte, mashing the vegetation in its mouth into a wet pulp. In a month that would bring twenty inches of rain, here was a brief lull, an opening of light, and the men's hearing adapted to the widening acoustics of the rainforest now that the constant drumming of water had ceased. The Marines listened to the surrounding jungle, the fine hairs of the inner ear attuned to the subtle shifts of tone the morning offered. Shade warblers and thicketbirds sang. They heard fruit doves and moorhens, honeyeaters and Woodford's rail. A drongo flew over, high above. Birds called out from the bamboo stands south of Mt Balbi. They sang in the floodplain forest and in the coconut groves, in the ancient limestone forests and along the river courses.

A Bougainville Monarch landed on a man's shoulder, but his focus was set beyond the green veil before him. He didn't notice the widening beauty of wings opening and closing on the belt of ammunition he carried. Behind the veil of leaves, the eyes of the Japanese officer blinked, quick as a bird startled from the brush. My grandfather swung his machete upward from left to right in a wide arc of metal that caught the man at the neckline, above the Adam's apple and just where the smooth column of the neck angles forward to the jawbone. The force of the blow lifted the man's face upward for a brief vision of leaves and sunlight before he staggered backward and fell into the green crush of the jungle.

Papa stumbled in the adrenaline and tunneling clarity of

that moment, the world around the two men blurred beyond recognition. His right foot caught in the snakelike roots of the tangled undergrowth and he almost fell over, on top of the Japanese officer, who was choking on his own blood, staring wild-eyed at my grandfather, while instinctively trying to unsheathe his katana from its scabbard.

I don't want to picture my grandfather quickly stepping on the man's wrist to pin it to his body as he swung the machete down and split the man's throat open wide across the jugular, a blow that turned his face sideways into the cool damp of the crumpled leaves. I'd rather Papa simply pause in the shock of the moment before slowly stepping back, the two of them staring at one another as the Japanese man relaxed his grip on the hilt of his sword.

Years back, when I was a boy of twelve, he unsheathed that machete and handed it to me, blade edge away. It was heavy and the metal surprised me with its warmth. A rough metal, with no polish and an unsharpened bevel. I held my grandfather's machete in both hands and lifted it carefully to examine it, the way the sacred is observed, eyes tracing the object with deliberation, slowly. This killed a man. For one Japanese officer, this was the key that opened the door into all that lies beyond.

Of course, the rifle reports, the cannon fire, the shells bursting
– the world in its patience takes them all under. By sand, by
wind, by erosion. By the steady labor of ruin. The creeper vine
hooks its bright tendrils and pulls history down into the earth.
The soldiers march on, though, generation by generation, one
war to another, through mud and rain and blistering sun. They
practice the principles of patrolling, they lock and load their
weapons, they feel the sickness in their stomachs and some
of them feel the dread in their chests as they cross the line of
departure, or worse still: they feel nothing at all, boredom
perhaps, routine, moving to contact, on radio silence, commu-
nicating with hand signals, gestures, a movement of the head,
a look of recognition in the eye.

The creeper vine hooks around their ankles and calves
with its green embrace. The creeper vine takes them all under.
The wind at their backs pushing them into the quiet spaces
of history, where names and lives and moments and words
and hopes and all manner of human beings are pulled down,
sand and water and the hard weight of what they've done
eventually turning them to stone.

I left the war in April 2004 and went home on leave. I'd turned in my weapon to the unit armorer and handed my ammo over to Bruzik. We were told to travel in civilian clothes, which I hadn't used in months. I wore Levis and a nondescript t-shirt, but kept my desert combat boots on. Just a short time before this, I'd put an Iraqi ex-sergeant major down on his knees in a rain-darkened street, put a sandbag over his head and wound duct tape around his skull, writing his 'target number' on the tape with a black-tipped Sharpie. I'd seen him shiver in fear as I did my job – a man we'd been told had planned and orchestrated the downing of a Chinook helicopter ferrying troops home for leave. And as I boarded the plane home, I closed my eyes and tried not to think of the possible weapons waiting in the darkness beyond the edge of the airfield.

We had a short layover in Bahrain, where the airport reminded me of shopping malls back home. Gleaming surfaces of tile and glass and marble given streams of vibrant light. Voices echoing down the corridors. Stores with shelves and display racks filled with colorful women's shoes – an assortment of empty flats, pumps, sandals. One of the other soldiers swayed out of a nearby lounge and leaned over as a pink column of vomit streamed from his mouth and splashed on the alabaster tile.

80

While I was headed home, the dead, too, made their journey back, in their body bags, radiating a kind of hushed and sacred presence. Hands lifting them, then lowering them into caskets. At 39,000 feet over the ocean, the rows of caskets are secured within the cold fuselage. And the dead lie with their heads toward the nose of the plane, their feet toward the cargo doors at the rear.

The crew chief keeps them company in the fuselage. He yawns before taking another swig of coffee from his Thermos. Red and white indicator lights on the panel above him flare in the lacquered polish of the caskets, tracing each smooth curve and edged line.

The planes bound for England have already landed. An honor guard stands to receive them on the tarmac. There is a procedure to this. There is a ritual. The dead sergeant will be in the lead hearse and his men will follow in a procession of black. When their loved ones stop near the Brize Norton memorial garden, family members will come forward to lay roses on the caskets. And those who will stand by the roadside, paying their respects as the funeral passes en route to the Oxford mortuary – some of them sleep with their lovers beside them now. And some of them sleep alone. Numbers glow soft and red in the face of the clock on the nightstand. One of them dreams she's dancing with her husband in the kitchen, years back, long before the surgeries and the setbacks and the words that pills and pain bring on. For now, it's 1966 in her head. December. And she's spinning. Her cream-colored skirt swirling out in a wide bell as they cross the kitchen floor. A needle in the groove bringing the orchestra to life around them.

When she wakes in the morning, she'll struggle to remember the dream as it fades. For a moment she'll think he's in bed again, and then she'll remember. She'll wipe the sleep from her eyes and exhale a long-held breath before reaching up to pull the cord that fills the lampshade with light.

81

Two flights later I found myself back home in Fresno, in a weird moving world of family, friends, strangers. America. I rented a car and took a road trip north along the western seaboard with Brian Voight, a man I'd known since I was a young boy, the two of us born four days apart and raised as brothers together in the San Joaquin Valley, California. We listened to Wilco and

Pink Floyd and Pavement and Black Rebel Motorcycle Club. Brian rolled joints along the way. We'd find a beach and he'd smoke them while I didn't talk about the war and we planned to start a new band when I finished with the army. And we kept our word: I survived, we made an album, and that same year Brian would die of stomach cancer. For the time being, we sat on the beach and watched the breakers rolling in. Talked about music and women and laughed about all that we'd shared over the years. As he wordlessly tried to remind me how to live, I didn't know that he would one day teach me how to die. He had a long year of dying in store for him. Multiple stents, like ports, emplaced on his chest and sides. Liter after liter of fluids drained. Fingertips turning from a jaundice-yellow to a hue of copper. I would find myself pouring his ashes into a wooden replica of a Viking longboat before setting the boat and sail on fire, the cloud of his remains seeking the lake bed in the waters he loved.

82

I drove to a rave party in Seattle. A misty rain. Sgt Gould and I purchasing tickets outside the gutted supermarket building. Our heads smooth and shaved, shoulders squared to all we met, walking in through the door to see a pink and furry six-foot-tall Energizer bunny rabbit cruising by on roller skates, replete with regulation-sized marching drum, thumping a drumhead with mallets. And as the rabbit did so, I saw a long-haired brunette wearing a leather bustier, thigh-high wet leather PVC boots, who smiled at me while pulling a man behind her by a leash cinched around his neck, the man wearing black leather Speedos.

Sgt Gould laughed, told me he was headed off toward the bar and the music, slapped me on the shoulder and said, 'Fucking dive in, man.'

There were ropes strung high above the old supermarket floor, from one support column to another. Long sheets were draped over the ropes to form streets for the bizarre carnival of souls on promenade. The hanging sheets also formed interior chambers, like the 'cuddle room' I entered then, a space furnished wholly with mattresses and pillows and soft blankets. Near the entrance where I left my shoes, a woman with only a sheet wrapped around her body sat beside a pile of books and wrote on a paper scroll. I nodded to her as I crawled in and worked my way past the prone bodies of lovers, past the woman who straddled a man and rode him slowly while reaching over to stroke off an older man who appeared to have sat down beside them simply to watch.

Music pulsed in my head. I lay down near a woman at the back of the room who stared up at the ceiling, smiling. She wore a perfume of jasmine and clove. The sheets smelled of smoke and eucalyptus, sweetgrass, bodies when they roll together in heat. I asked her name and she told me it wouldn't make a difference. This wasn't a matter of love, she said. This was a kind of medicine that most likely wouldn't work. Sheets for the bandaging. A damn sad thing, she said. And then she leaned in close, her lips at the lobe of my ear, her breath tingling my skin. And as she caressed the back of my smooth skull, she whispered, 'I'm going to draw my husband from you now. Touch by touch, I will bring him back into this world.'

83

The war itself is on television. It plays on muted screens in airports across the country, a *threat level orange* script scrolling from right to left beneath plumes of smoke, soldiers wandering in the aftermath of a bomb, pointing at unknowable things offscreen, while officers speak to America without realising the volume of their voices has been lowered below the ambient noise of the rooms they have traveled so far to address.

The war hovers over cocktail shakers, bamboo muddlers, rabbit bars and cocktail strainers at the Plough & Stars on Clement Street. The war hovers its medevac helicopters over bourbon and gin, tonic and bitters at the 500 Club on Guerrero in the Mission District. Broken ammo crates and dunnage from the mortar pits overflows from the trash bins out back. Regulars sit at their stools and sip their drinks as they watch the war illuminated scene by scene before them. I piss into the urinal, surrounded by graffiti and the night's beery stench, swaying with alcohol.

I dropped Brian off back in Fresno and headed to San Francisco to catch up with another life-long friend, Stacey Lynn Brown. She told me prior to my deployment that she'd be willing to drive over my foot so that I wouldn't have to go. She'd signed on to act as literary executor of my estate were I to die in Iraq. I'd also given her power of attorney and she took on all of my bills and taxes while I was in combat.

We promptly went to Biscuits & Blues, an upscale Cajun restaurant and bar, where Tyrin Benoit & the Shuckers played songs from their first album, *Sometimes It Takes Awhile* . . . I remember a roadie getting up on stage to play spoons on a washboard hung from his neck, and, most of all, a dark-haired Syrian woman who I wanted to go to bed with before, during and after shrimp and grits, a basket of biscuits and several rounds of vodka in Old-Fashioned glasses.

We ended up hanging out with the band afterward. Stacey got stoned with the rest of the band while I sat against a wall with the guitarist, who turned out to have been a Marine back in the First Gulf War. 'You watch yourself out there, brother. Don't give 'em anything to shoot at.'

I recuperated with a Bloody Mary the next morning, but my hangover didn't stop the war from reverberating through my head. The shit has hit the fan in my absence, bridges and roadways in the center of the country have been blown, the supply routes, from north to south, are effectively cut in half. An uprising in Najaf pulls my unit down to the outskirts of the city. Troops massing there for what might turn into an enormous battle, house-to-house and block-by-block fighting – this is what the TV journalist tells us may be imminent for the troops outside and for the Iraqis inside Najaf. I slide sunglasses onto my face and walk out of the bar into the morning light of California. Feel the breeze coming in off the ocean. I lean up against the brick side of a building while Stacey lights a Winston. And I don't tell her that I'm thinking about Jax and Fiorillo and Bosch. I don't tell her how I'm feeling guilty for the cool breeze and the unfolding of the day before me, how relieved I am to be in America, with her, and how much of a coward I am. It goes without saying. The silence of John Wayne, but not the hero. And so I just breathe in the cool air. Listen to passing conversations. Music unraveling from a car traveling through the intersection. Accordion doors sliding upward as a business starts the day.

A rocket-propelled grenade will pass right by Zapata just a few hours from now, and I won't know anything about it until I get back to the war. The company will be headed south, driving through a linear ambush in the dark. Zapata will lean forward in the hatch to empty a magazine into the darkness and he'll tell me afterward that the men who were firing at him stopped firing altogether. I'll imagine dead men lying in the dark. And he'll tell me that his wife left him, too. Something he found out by email while I was gone. 'Married one day and then, well, fuck, everything goes to shit.'

85

In the spaces between moments, in the gaps of memory, I'm sleeping. Or I'm staring out a window at the afternoon traffic. Sunlight flaring and sliding off metal surfaces traveling at 35, 45, 80 mph. Strangers blur from one to another as they negotiate the crowded sidewalks. Some of them gesturing. Their faces worn and exhausted by the afternoon. I think they could all stop where they are in order to close their eyes and dream while the stoplights shift from green to yellow to red. Or I'm standing at a counter while the person at the register stops to look at me when she realises that I'm somewhere far away and the world is incredibly loud inside my head. She points to the objects on the counter and says, enunciating her words more slowly, 'Sir, would you like paper or plastic?'

Each day is a day a sniper can't view me in a scope, the crosshairs aiming at my ribcage or my groin or the midline crease of my upper lip. It's a day when a bullet can't puncture the philtrum to shatter my upper jawbone and travel through the cavern of speech to ricochet off the bony interior surface of the spinal cord, leaving me coughing and sputtering my own blood on a dirt road as shadows lean over calling out my own name to me, saying, 'You're gonna make it, Sgt T, hang in there, buddy. Keep talking to him – keep him awake.' Each day is a day without artillery shells fashioned into road-side bombs. Or grenades. Or mortars. Or vehicle rollovers. Or drownings. These are the days I can subtract from the war.

86

When I mention these things to Stacey, years later, as a way of apologising for my silence, she says:

Actually, you did tell me. I asked you why you were scanning the rooftops of Berkeley and you told me you couldn't stop – that if you let your guard down while here, your men might die when you got back over there. In fact, you Xeroxed your journal so I would understand what was happening to you – so that someone, somewhere, would know what was happening to you. You marveled at concrete beneath your feet instead of sand. Silverware instead of sporks. I tried my hardest to keep you grounded and focused and tethered to this world I prayed you would return to. You told me it was dangerous to stay in this world. That you had to stay where you were and take your chances. I told you that was unacceptable. That this world was waiting for you. All you had to do was return to us. To it. To me.

87

When I dropped Stacey off at the departure's terminal in San Francisco, I could feel time's insistent cruelty working to undo our curbside embrace. I remember thinking, if I let go of her, I let go of a world, a way of living, a life.

88

A couple of days before Stacey boarded the plane, we went to the Circus Center – a flying trapeze school near Golden Gate Park. Instructors clapped chalk dust from their hands and when they spoke their words echoed through the expansive interior of the gym. I sat on the blue mats by the wall and watched as Stacey learned, high over the sloping nets below, how to let go of the trapeze bar at the apex of her swing so that the world might pause at a few minutes after 11 a.m, the clockface suspended by it, cars and motorcycles and city buses in the roadway beyond us fixed in place as molecules within the construction of the moment vibrated at a constant rate, while Stacey, her body in dialogue with the laws of gravity and the laws of motion, untethered herself from the constraints of this world to rise into the oxygen of this century, flying.

I sat on the blue mat and did not climb the ladder to that high state because I knew that I could hurt myself in the process. I knew that I could damage what was, in essence, an item in the inventory of the US Army. My body, volunteered.

89

At the end of my leave, I met up with Brian Voight again – this time to go four-wheeling in the Sierra Nevada Mountains east of Fresno. Snow covered the ground from a recent storm and the daytime temperature was cool enough to prevent large sheets of ice on some of the back roads from melting. Of course, with time running short and a plane to catch back to my unit, we managed to get his Jeep stuck in a snow bank. As we maneuvered around the vehicle, we both fell on the ice – hard enough to knock the wind out of Brian, both of us sliding downhill, laughing by the time we came to a stop. Afterward, we tried digging the tires out, placing a bundle of broken tree limbs in the wheel ruts to help the tires catch, but they just kept spinning and digging themselves deeper, transforming each rut into a hardened well of ice. Brian lit a cigarette and we stood atop the snow bank, considering our options. The winch on the front bumper had cable, but no longer worked. We debated whether it would be worth stretching out the cable and tethering it to the tree anyways.

It seemed as if the earth itself were doing its best to keep me home – the San Joaquin Valley, the Sierra Nevada Mountains, the boulders carved from the mountain long ago, the ancient redwoods towering above, all doing their best to delay me from returning to the arms' room where an M4 awaited my return.

Grandma Anna kept a secret photo album of military servicemen she'd danced with in San Francisco during the Second World War – men on leave and those headed to war. I used to visit her at the old house in Fresno and she'd often sit beside me as we pored over albums while Papa drank from a pint of whiskey stowed in the tool shed out back.

'Now this one here,' she'd say, leaning toward me, 'he had the biggest crush on Lorene.' Lorene was her younger sister, my great-aunt.

Each turn of the page brought a new series of small black and white portrait photos of men in uniform whose names she couldn't recall, or chose not to say, though the pad of her index finger would sometimes linger over a photograph here and there. It was in these moments I could hear strains of Benny Goodman and Tommy Dorsey tunes in the air around us.

In one of the photos, Anna wears a blue skirt, the color of an April afternoon, with a soft white blouse, white as a nurse's uniform, as she smiles beside Lorene in a tree-lined park. She often worked as a part-time model in San Francisco, and photographs of her were displayed in shopfront windows throughout the city. For the dances, though, she'd have simple headshots done in wallet-sized duplicates that she could exchange with the servicemen she met.

I thought of the many islands in the Pacific where her photo may have traveled and of the many conditions her photograph may have endured. Anna's face, smiling at young weary men who were to meet the grenade or bayonet. Or, perhaps a Japanese soldier held her photo in his fingertips, the way one holds something delicate and profound and unknowable, while sitting quietly by himself after the attack. The Japanese soldier tells no one, not even his wife, that he carries this photo with him throughout the duration of the war, which, after months of recuperation in a hospital waiting for a wounded leg to heal, ended, leaving several more months of bandages and phantom pain. My grandmother with him the entire time.

91

It's April 2004. American servicemen take the twenty-minute train into the Centraal Station from Schiphol airport. Country boys from Wisconsin and Illinois, city boys from Birmingham and Honolulu – all of them with an eight-hour layover in Amsterdam. They wander the canals and narrow alleys of the Rossebuurt past the Erotic Museum and the Oude Kerk, past the closed morning doors of the Banana Club and Theatre Casa Rosso. They weave their way between bicycle messengers and the Nigerian pushers who loiter by the bridges, hawking in low whispers, saying, 'Rock, man? You want rock?' The tourists and unemployed stoned before noon in the coffee shops. Young women from Bratislava and Warsaw and small towns in Eastern Europe I've never heard of tap on the display windows and coax the young men inside.

I am no exception.

She knows I'm a soldier headed back to war. It's easy enough to see it written on my face. The way I lie down. The death of me in her hands, a ritual I don't fully comprehend. A dying man, extinguished in the flight from home. A man who is also simply returning to a place that feels more real than home. For a moment I feel the heat rising within me and I am close to being alive again, before falling back into a landscape of bullets and mortars and fear and adrenaline and boredom. Her dark brown hair framed her face in shadow as she rode me on the thin mattress. A warm red light filled the room. She spoke to me in Dutch as she rode on, a few words of English I can't remember now. Our faces were very close and I could feel her breath on my lips. The room was a perfume of sweat and body oil, with the faint sweet trace of a flower I couldn't name.

When I think back on it, it seems more like a scene from an emergency room. The red lights flaring. Me, lying on a gurney with a blue cotton sheet folded over a thin mattress. A nurse helping me breathe, her body rising and falling as she applies the defibrillator paddles to shock my heart back into this world.

After I dressed and paid and staggered back out into the clamor of Amsterdam, I sat at the bar in the Casa Rosso to watch a stripper bring a shy man from the audience up on stage with her. She sat him in a simple chair and teased him with a brief lap dance while I bought a beer on tap. She then had him stand while she sat in the chair and lifted her skirt to reveal a small bright triangle of material, like a small flag, partially stuffed into her vagina. The man demurred at first, but she urged and goaded him into reaching down to pull it out. The audience fell silent for a moment as the man pulled the flag out, only to realise that what he held was a series of multi-colored flags attached to a single cord. In fact, as she encouraged him to return to his seat back in the third row of bleacher-like seating, we all watched as each flag emerged from inside her, in blues and oranges, reds and purples and greens. She then blew him a kiss, reeled in her colorful pennant rope, and bowed before grabbing her chair and leaving the stage for the main act.

This is when a man and woman walked onto the stage dressed like a sailor and a Dutch farm girl from a bygone age. The music cued and a smoky-voiced woman sang a slow cabaret tune in French. As servers delivered drinks to patrons in the terraced seats, the onstage couple undressed and soon enough advanced from kissing to fondling to fellatio to the woman positioning herself on all fours facing away from her partner – he held his cock steady as she pressed herself back onto him and fully anchored him into her. The choreography was impeccable. I stayed to watch the next show, not realising that the performances cycled and repeated throughout the day. The professionalism of their act was mimicked down to the last detail. A nipple sucked. A quick spank here, a scratched back there. And I realised then that I carried a desire within me that was equal in measure to the floorshow's gestures toward the infinite, something circular, something repetitive, a tether cinched fast to something deep in the well of memory.

94

Soon enough, I'll find myself in a shower stall on a base in a war zone. Water streaming down, water articulating the curves of my body, defining the available surface for light and shadow. And in my imagination, with each shower, the armature of my body in conversation with the imagined body of a lover. Mechanical and choreographed. Set to a timer. I'll dry off and wrap the towel around my waist, step out of the shower to turn on the faucet in front of me. All the mirrors remain affixed to the wall in a long row above their individual sinks. The mirrors will be fogged up. I will wipe the ridge of my palm across the cool surface of the mirror, and, for a brief moment before the fog returns, I'll recognise the man staring back at me.

The first few days after I rejoin my unit, I feel like a different version of myself, a stranger, a cherry. The overpasses and bridges blown during the uprising while I was gone have been temporarily spanned with engineer bridges and pontoon bridges, tanks stationed at each end. I duck down inside the hatch at the first roadside bomb after my return, and I hesitate in the hull, failing to rise and fire at the flat desert landscape adjacent to the roadway. I don't *shoot at any known or suspected enemy target*. I freeze.

Given a few more days, a few more missions – the routine of the war sinks back in. We spend several weeks away from Mosul, running convoy escort for the supply train through Baghdad. Our sole purpose is to protect eighteen-wheelers carrying supplies north and south along the central corridor through the ancient city. Each morning we wake early – either at a supply depot south of Baghdad, where we sleep in the parking lot and I string up a hammock and drape myself in netting to ward off the sandflies; or we wake north of the city at a huge base, Camp Taji, where we've thick old dusty-orange Bedouin tents to sleep in.

I see the scorch marks on the highway where vehicles have been left to burn as convoys plowed through ambushes and indirect attacks. Bosch describes how I missed the day kids had thrown a piece of rebar into the oncoming windshield of a big rig with a Filipino driver at the wheel, a civilian contractor who wore a blue flak vest and a blue helmet. The driver jack-knifed at 45 mph on the highway and the vehicle lurched sideways, crashing down on the driver's side – the windshield imploding and a jagged shard of glass slicing open the man's throat. 'He bled out in about ninety seconds,' Bosch says.

96

The attacks continued after I arrived. We drove through them. Snipers from a building in the distance. A van stopping high above us at a huge, LA-style freeway interchange, sliding its doors open to strafe our convoy with a machine gun before driving off into the city. Bruzik yelling, 'Close the hatches' whenever mortars lobbed airburst rounds at us – rounds designed to detonate above, spraying shrapnel downward.

At some point an officer declared over the battalion net: 'You are authorised to shoot children.' Bruzik stepped off to the side with me and said, with his voice low so our squad couldn't hear him, 'Dude. I don't think I can shoot children.' He stopped looking at the ground and looked me in the eye.

'Just stand high in the hatch and pump your shotgun. Shoot a beanbag at them if they keep coming.* It won't reach them, anyways, but they don't know that. They'll see you pump the shotgun and start running, most likely.'

97

Guarding the supply train through Baghdad, we stuck to our Rules of Engagement. These included denying civilian vehicles access into our convoys. They'd have to wait for us to pass, which forced Iraqi drivers to sit idling in traffic. They'd often try to pull in and drive to wherever they were headed, but our Strykers would slam into them and push them out of the convoy's path. Nineteen tons of metal, armament, intention. Our drivers and vehicle commanders kept a kind of informal daily count of the cars they'd hit during each convoy. The highest number I heard from one of the drivers was eight. During one of these hits, Sgt Zapata was up in the hatch. A Stryker in front of us had just slammed into a vehicle trying to enter the roadway at a busy marketplace with pedestrians milling around. He saw the car flipped onto its passenger side, pinning one or more people underneath it. He saw the crowd rush to pull the car off. And he watched as a man with a distant expression

---

*A beanbag is a non-lethal munition.

leaned against a nearby wall, part of his scalp peeled back from his forehead, skin and hair dangling behind him. And, as we drove on, Zapata saw the man reach to smooth the flap back into place.

98

While the drivers used our vehicles to dominate the roadway, those of us standing in the rear hatches warned off civilians by other means. When a car began to approach us as if it meant to pass, I'd raise my M4 up in the air, the barrel toward Mars. If the car continued, I'd step up onto the troop seat below to make myself as visible as possible to the driver, before lowering the barrel of my weapon and training it on the car.

We'd use multiple hand gestures to warn the driver to slow down. But if they kept coming, I'd fire. I'd lean into the weapon and fire two shots into the radiator. The car would then slow and pull over to the shoulder of the road, or decelerate rapidly, then disappear as we drove on. I stopped counting the cars we shot at each day. I got tired of counting.

99

We are told that in another convoy someone has dropped a land mine from an overpass and managed to kill two American soldiers. This is the same day a civilian car drives up alongside one of the Strykers and explodes, knocking a platoon sergeant unconscious and lodging shrapnel into another soldier's neck. While aid was rendered to the wounded soldiers, I looked out over the summer asphalt with its waves of rolling heat, the roadway fuming for as far as I could see, and I observed the distance the explosive force had launched the mangled engine of the bomber's vanished car.

100

In a large movie theater at Camp Taji, once the site of an Iraqi Republican Guard unit, I watched Brad Pitt sprint across the sand between two nations to launch himself with a spear aimed at his enemy, Hector.

After the movie, we walked to the Morale, Welfare and Recreation tent, or MWR, by the commissary. I bought a paperback copy of Michael Moore's *Fahrenheit 911* and a package of beef jerky. I think Bruzik walked out with a bag stuffed with cigarettes and fuck mags like *FHM* and *Maxim*, as well as the latest issue of *Soldier of Fortune*. Jax finished up his phone call home and we caught a bus across base to return to the cloth-bound heat of the orange Bedouin-style tents. A mortar fell from the high angle of hell not long after that – a direct hit between the commissary and the tent where soldiers called home from a crudely built plywood bank of phones. Quick-thinking soldiers ran into the commissary to grab tampons, t-shirts – anything they could get their hands on to stop the flow of blood from those lying in the dirt, unconscious or calling out in pain.

Other soldiers stood by, staring. Some pulled out cameras to take photographs.

Taped to the doors of the enormous chow hall on that same base, a sign announced the following: *Wednesday Nite/ Open Mic/ Poetry Nite!*

Poetry. The idea that soldiers might gather on an improvised stage to read poems in Iraq – it didn't seem plausible, or real. I wrote poems in my notebooks and I read poetry when I had time, but I felt alone in that process. In many ways, the language of journal entries and poetry forged an internal space within me, a space that didn't belong to the army or to the community of soldiers I served with. Sgt Turner was too small of a space for a human being to live in.

I couldn't imagine sharing those words there, aloud, in Iraq. But as I write these words, Hemingway's bullshit detector pings. Maybe it was more selfish than that. Maybe I just didn't want to show how vulnerable and sensitive and afraid I was, how deeply the word *beauty* intertwines with the words *love* and *loss*. That's it. Vanity and embarrassment. Cowardice. I was afraid to admit that I loved this world. I was afraid to admit that I was alive.

The sign taped to those doors seemed like a message from some other place, some other time.

102

And then it was time for Mosul again.

Bosch played nerve solitaire with a boot knife. He no longer talked about saving up enough money to go to film school, the reason he'd joined the army in the first place. I sat across from him in the chow hall and ate lasagna, watched the tip of the blade lift and fall between his splayed fingers.

After the latest mortar landed, after the explosion, after the initial run into the concrete bunker that served as our overhead cover – Bruzik yelled, 'Grab the aid bag!' I chucked him the bag and he ran on ahead as I struggled to keep up, my old ankle surgery slowing me down.

The Turkish cook lay prostrate on the dirt road near the camp perimeter. His two friends, fellow cooks from the dining facility, stood nearby, their bodies bending at the waist a little, pressing their hands hard into their stomachs and then raising them to their mouths, their fingers opening then closing to white-knuckled fists as they gathered the Turkish escaping from their lips the way those in trauma sometimes do – struggling to keep from announcing to the world all that their eyes tell them is true.

The cook foamed at the mouth. His eyes began to join the cloud layer in the stratosphere above. The shrapnel lodged in the back of his skull had punctured through bone to split the soft matter of the brain somewhere deep within the convoluted house of memory.

Another soldier reached him before us and was attempting to render aid. But it was obviously too late. A mechanic was there, too, kicking open an Israeli stretcher while still wearing a welding hood with the visor flipped up.

The cook now found himself in Istanbul, and the streets of Istanbul had buckled and twisted until the roadway split open. Shopfront windows on Istiklâl Caddesi exploded outward in shards as pedestrians scrambled to regain their footing, some of them screaming, some of them staring at the broken world in disbelief. Beyond the dome of the Blue Mosque and the pink walls of the Hagia Sophia, the Bosphorus itself had been rent in two. People on the shoreline watched in horror as the waters sank into the depths of the splitting earth, sheared away, their mouths opened in silence as they watched the Asian side of Istanbul rise up, the laws of gravity and physics undone before them, the way one might pull a small tree from the ground by its roots and lift it; it rose into the clouds, which parted, and then disappeared into the vast blue reaches of sky beyond.

The dying man stood near the Blue Mosque. He could hear the call to Azan broadcasting from speakers high up in the minarets, echoed minaret by minaret throughout the city. His wife and daughter ran toward him from across the road, but just as they entered the street the earth shook and buckled once more and they began to rise over the pavement, like strange swimmers in light or featherless birds they rose, higher and higher, as he stood there and watched them disappear.

As we tried to stanch the blood and a Humvee arrived to cart him off to the 'Cash', blood began to flow through cracks into the streets and parks of Istanbul.* It flooded everything, spilling into the flowerbeds, spreading through the relics and statues and exhibits at the Archeological Museum, where Polyhymnia placed a finger to her lips and fell silent. The Alexander sarcophagus overturned and blood coated its insides. Blood poured into the old Basilica Cistern beneath the city, where the column pedestal of Medusa's marble head stared through the warm fluid at the wide eyes of fish, who turned to stone and sank finally to their ruin. The widening river of blood ran through bathhouses and bookstores; it ran through the streets and poured through the windows to flood the homes and businesses where people lived and worked; it overtook cars as their drivers and passengers sat frozen in shock. The blood began to fill the harem's quarters in the Topkapi Palace, then, and it overturned carts of fabrics and spices and gold in the Grand Bazaar, where tourists cried out in whatever language they knew that this must surely be the end of the world.

And the dying man knew it. His mouth continued to foam open as we stood over him, lifting him and lowering him carefully onto the stretcher that would take him away. When I looked in his eyes, seagulls circled the beautiful dome of the Blue Mosque and, for a moment, the call to Azan rang through the curving horns of his ears.

_____

*CASH: Combat Army Support Hospital.

In the early evenings, when the sky's hues would shift in the falling light, I liked to watch the bats rise from their roosts in abandoned homes throughout the city to gather by the hundred along the river and out in the eucalyptus groves. As the dusk came in, our platoon sometimes conducted counter-mortar missions in one of the grand old parks. Our Strykers positioned themselves in the grass-covered berms of Saddam's former tank emplacements while our squads fanned out to create a perimeter in the wood line. I remember one of our interpreters, Jargis, who was roughly forty-five, maybe fifty, and how he liked to tell stories. He slowly gestured with his flattened palm, taking in the park. 'In the old days, the couples liked to come here, to, you know, fuck each other. This was the Love Park.'

We laughed, but tried to keep our laughter down so the platoon sergeant wouldn't walk over and chew us out.

'And I sometimes come out here – the grass was sometimes high, you know, and the couples would be out here, kissing,' he said, motioning around us, 'even here, right here.' I tried to imagine the sunlight and the grass, the tank emplacements erased, lovers embracing each other, kissing. 'And I like to sneak on them, with my camera.'

A slow sly smile spread across Fiorillo's face, and he

stretched out the vowel as he said, 'Whaaaaaat?' raising the pitch of his voice some.

'I tell you true. I tell you true. I had the video-camera and the men sometimes would chase me. Angry, you know? They chase me to my car.'

As the guys laughed, I pictured Jargis running through the waist-high grass holding his camcorder in the air, pursued by an angry lover who slowed as he fumbled to zip up his pants and gather his senses in the daylight.

I often wonder if Jargis survived, if he's still alive. One of the rumors we heard was that twelve of the interpreters we worked with had their heads cut off once we left.

Our platoon often dispersed to set up observation posts in abandoned homes. We'd sit tired and bored inside. A soldier would prop up an old scaffolding board in one of the interior hallways downstairs to practice throwing his knife, gauging the balance and heft of the metal in his fingertips before flipping it end over end toward the target. The neighborhood generator operator often cursed, I thought, banging at the machine inside its sweatbox of a shack. Occasional traffic passed by on its way to whatever a normal life might look like for a citizen of Mosul at the time. As I walked the empty rooms of those houses and sat staring through window frames for hours on end at my sector of the city, I wondered if the owners were in Jordan or Sweden or in Kurdish northern Iraq. I wondered if they were dead. I pictured a family in a refugee camp on the Syrian border. Crouched over a small cook fire. Dogs barking in the distance. A man sharing a cigarette with another, the smoke disappearing quickly in the blue dusk. The silence between them as they consider who walks through the rooms of their lives in the hours before dawn.

106

A carbine in my hands. A bone microphone on my forehead.* Winter stars above.

The Iraqi driver is experiencing a pain beyond any I've ever known. He has an injury shaped like a horseshoe crushed into his forehead and his infant child cries in his wife's arms. It's dark out and I can't see any of this. I'm trying to figure out what just happened. The headlights in the roadway. The car that managed to get past me; the car I was supposed to stop. The step to my left that saved me. The torqued sound of metal on metal, ruckling.

---

* A bone microphone is part of a tactical headset which features a microphone pressed against the bones of the user's skull to pick up sound.

Doc High tends to the injured man, kneeling beside him on the roadbed, aid kit opened, his hands quick and sure. Another soldier holds an M4 over them with the tac light on, illuminating the scene. And when the injured Iraqi man asks why Doc High speaks to him in a foreign language, our interpreter reassures him that it's okay, that he's a doctor and that he's speaking in Latin. This seems to soothe the man somewhat; the interpreter recognised the injured man would be more frightened if he thought the men crouched over and treating him were Americans. I don't remember him saying much after this, though the baby kept crying in its mother's arms somewhere in the darkness beyond the cone of light.

I never forgive myself for *not* having shot this man.

My hands, shaking.

107

In a Facebook message, Doc High says:

It wasn't a horseshoe-shaped injury. He had fractures horizontally across his face as a result of face-planting into the slat armor [the metal cage around our Stryker designed to fend off RPG attacks]. This caused his brain to bleed [and] the unequal pupils I saw. He had what's called intra-cranial pressure. Without top-notch medical care, he more than likely did expire.

We moved twenty kilometers south-east of Mosul to hold a company-sized firebase for a few weeks as the other unit headed south on some unknown mission.

It was a tiny firebase, with a large, squat, two-story building at its center which once served as an agricultural college. I called it the Overlook Hotel. The building was sandbagged on all sides and deadly black snakes, desert cobras, nested in the sandbags. We were undermanned and those we were fighting knew it: an informant notified us of an impending attack to overrun our camp. We were told that two hundred men were being assembled for the attack and that they had already prepared the improvised terrain models we called sand tables as part of their operational planning. I was immediately struck by that last note: *sand tables*. We were fighting against formally trained soldiers. I began to imagine what it would be like when they breached the compound and we were forced to retreat floor by floor up to the rooftop.

The mortar rounds started falling from two different firing points shortly after dark. Our machine-gun crew returned fire from the rooftop, but the cannon flashes near the river were well out of range. The platoon leader stayed cool. My squad stood in full 'battle rattle' in the interior hallway of the building, just outside the platoon command post, while something inside me began to unravel and snap. The rest of the soldiers in the squad stood in silence along the wall – I began pacing back and forth, talking aloud to myself, and to no one, and toward the command post. 'Let's fucking *go*. Let's just fucking *go* already.' And when we got the word and ran to the vehicle with its ramp already down, and as we rolled out and skirted the village of Hamman al-Alil, I continued to curse and shout from up in the hatch. I yelled at the homes we passed. I cursed at the drapes covering their windows. I cursed at their closed doors. I shouted at their unmoving palm trees, their vacant streets, the solid unmoving nature of all I saw before me. A Blackhawk fired two Hellfire missiles at the suspected mortar position ahead of us. I saw the smoky white shock wave of the missiles in their downward trajectory. Lightning discharged into the earth. And I heard the explosions. I watched as immediately afterward the night's reverence gathered a renewed darkness around the damage. And though I stopped cursing and yelling at the world around me, transfixed by what I saw, I was not satisfied.

Back at the base, the platoon sergeant rouses anybody racked out and not on duty to line up in the interior hallway. Most of us blink and stand against the wall in our shorts and flip-flops, swaying with a half-dream, half-groggy, god-dammit why-am-I-fucking-standing-here-awake look. The platoon sergeant fumes and steams at the dark end of the hall.

We cast sideways glances at one another and wait to hear what this is all about.

'Let me tell you something, men. I do not even know where to fucking begin. I do not,' he repeats, this time a staggered emphasis overtaking him, as if placing a period after each word – 'I do not know where to begin.' We look sideways at one another again: this is something new. 'But I'll tell you what – I'm sure as hell gonna figure this out right here and right fucking now.' He walks out of the dark end of the hallway, pacing past us, staring at each soldier. 'No one is going anywhere – let me repeat – no one is going anywhere until I find out who the fuck dropped a load in the urinal tonight.' He paused while we tried to comprehend the bizarre world we were living in. Dell laughed, then held his hand over his mouth. 'Let me correct that: no one's going anywhere until I find out who the sorry mother-fucker is that dropped a fucking *brick* in the goddamn urinal. I mean, who does that? Who the fuck does that?'

I don't remember how long this went on, but we spent an interminable period listening to his rant. And then the whole thing was inexplicably settled when Shovlin, quite possibly the dumbest soldier in the United States Army, spoke up, though meekly, saying, 'It could've been me, Sergeant. I sometimes do things when I sleep.'

110

On patrol, some of the soldiers piss into plastic bottles and then screw the caps back on tight. As we drive through a small cluster of mud-walled homes, children chase after us with their hands gesturing for something to drink. I watch the children scramble to recover the piss lobbed their way as some of the bottles roll and spin once they hit the dirt shoulder, others bursting open to vent a spray of urine.

111

We dropped ramps and most of the platoon set out on foot to touch base with the local police station. I stayed as a guard in the radio hatch at the back of my squad's Stryker. There were three other Strykers – we patrolled back and forth on a wide, residential boulevard connecting two traffic circles.

We must have completed this circuit about eight times. I had just seen a gorgeous Iraqi woman walking along the main boulevard. I was looking down one of the side streets spoking out from the traffic circle when I heard the distinctive sound. Not the *thunk* I'd read about – I didn't hear that – but, rather, the high-pitched sizzling as it flew.

I pause to consider the round itself: spinning. The way a bird stabilises itself in the flight over water, wings in their downward motion, breathing, filling its lungs with oxygen, then rising again in conversation with the air. I like to imagine the round shining as it spun, sunlight caught in the angles of metal and cast outward at a speed too fast for the eye.

Quicker than I could formulate the letters R-P-G, I knew what it was and that it was behind me. And it was a great shot. A direct hit. Right in line with me. One moment I was standing at name-tape defilade on the seat cushions of the troop hold scanning the street in front of me and thinking about a beautiful woman, my upper torso and head visible to those outside, and then: the properties of the physical world shifted. Boots slipped from their station, my eye taking in my weapon with its barrel pointed up at the sky; I could see the blue world framed in the circle of the open hatch. And I fell down, down into the troop hold, thinking, *Why can't I stop this? Why do I keep falling?*

Bruzik picked up a jagged piece of the exploded material afterward as the platoon mounted up and left.

And the man who placed the launcher on his shoulder and pulled the trigger to welcome me into the land of the dead, he remembers the perfect flight of the rocket as it traveled between us. He remembers the sound of that explosion and the slow-motion fall of my body into the cold green box of the vehicle. That troop hold. That birdcage where the owl calls out for water.

Sgt Turner is dead.

I was there when it happened. I climbed back up from inside the troop hold to stand in the hatch as our driver juiced it and we sped away from the explosion.

My head ringing. The multi-story buildings were still standing, brown and drab and without light. The cloud cover remained. And there in the street where the RPG struck, the dead Sgt Turner stood up, holding his head in his hands as he did so, swaying in the dust and exhaust fumes. He recedes and diminishes in my field of vision as we drive further and further away.

I'll imagine him wandering around that traffic circle when I'm back in my hooch, lying on my rack. He walks one of the wide boulevards of Mosul for hours, walking until the boulevard narrows, its meridian replaced with painted lines faded with age and use, walking until the avenue becomes a smaller road and then the drive shifts to a simple dirt lane, far from the shrapnel and the shouting he came from, so that he might rest on the banks of the Tigris, where the vast assembly of the dead have gathered before him.

The dead press their way through the elephant grass and papyrus thickets, wordless as they wade into the river. The water gives slightly and they sink for a moment before rising again, buoyant and light, to drift in the shallows just offshore. Seagulls wheel and turn in the air above, crying out from time to time – they see the dead lining the banks and filling the river. Hundreds of thousands, perhaps. More. As far as the eye can see.

And some of them pause to watch Sgt Turner as he makes his way down to the water's edge. He takes off his black gloves, unlaces his desert boots and sets them beside him. He pulls the Velcro flap on his Kevlar vest and lays it folded by his boots. He pulls his chinstrap down slightly to slide his helmet off, setting it on the flak vest with its plates of body armor. When he unrolls his boot socks from the ankle downward and off, the faint trace of the breeze cools the pads of his feet. Some of the dead harden their gaze as Sgt Turner parts the tall grass and wades into the river. Some of the dead stare off toward the city skyline.

Blackhawks fly in wide tandem circles, their distant rotor-blades rolling deep and low over the water, like drums.

Sgt Turner leans his head back into the cool gray surface of the river until his ears fully submerge. High winds erase the contrails of fighter jets in the stratosphere above as he listens to the muted wavelengths of sound the water carries out to sea.

When he rolls his head to the side and looks toward the shore, he sees a small boy crouching there, staring at him. The expression on the boy's face is as gray and reflective as the river. There is something stilled and aged in the boy. And as the boy looks on, Sgt Turner closes his eyes and sinks under the water's surface.

The battle is over.

It is 1862, and in a forest clearing near Sharpsburg, Maryland, Antietam has turned into a vast landscape of recovery, loss and burial.

The fouled barrels of the day's ordnance turned silent. Rifles cleaned and stacked in distant bivouacs. The horses for the artillery trains unhitched from their caissons and fed from sacks of rough-cut oats on a roadside somewhere beyond the far hills. The day's sweat has been brushed from their smooth coats and blankets draped over them for the night ahead.

Two men – Clem Jessups and a man known only as O'Reilly – pause under the wide branches of an oak, staring into the moonlit tableau before them. They can smell the smoke from the campfires drifting in from across the riverbank in the distance. Mist hovers in a white layer just over the tops of the corn stubble in the clearing beyond the trees. The two men wait in the shadows. O'Reilly is about to say something, but Clem shushes him with the back of his hand held up in the air between them, his index finger pointing upward, as if to say, 'There – you hear that?'

'Just a 'coon,' O'Reilly whispers with a tone that rises some. More question than statement.

'Maybe. Maybe so.'

Clem pauses a moment longer before motioning them forward, a low-voiced 'Let's get on with it, then' spoken as he steps into the cornfield. They move slowly, deliberately, feeling their way through the cornfield with each boot gliding forward and set down firmly before moving the trailing foot. The moon-light helps, but still O'Reilly nearly stumbles over the first body he comes upon. 'Here's one.' He takes the pliers from his sack and kneels down to begin the task of opening the dead man's mouth and pulling the upper and lower teeth from the jawbone. Clem taught him how to do it right.

'You pull the tooth behind the incisor first. Like this. See? Doesn't have to be done clean. Just get it out. That'll give you some wiggle room for working the rest of them out of the bone.' And O'Reilly had taken to it. The main thing was to give a slight twist and develop a feel for when the root breaks at the jawbone itself. The tooth would pop out after that. Easy. Quick.

The men worked in silence, dropping the teeth in small burlap sacks hung around their necks by a cord. O'Reilly thought that this was probably the easiest they'd had it so far. In fact, the first time he'd walked onto a battlefield and pulled a dead man's tooth was likely under the worst conditions he'd experienced up to this point. It was raining, dark out, not long before dawn. Cold. The soldier had been torn apart by some-thing fierce and he lay in a low and grassy swale. O'Reilly's boots sunk ankle-deep in the mud, pools of icy water rising in the tracks behind him.

Not resurrectionists, Clem and O'Reilly were following a trade well established by this point in history. Teeth had been collected on the battlefields of the Peninsular War and the War of 1812, long before this new war. In fact, barrels of those teeth had been sent to American dentists for the dentures they made. The teeth taken from the dead at Waterloo became so popular in Europe that for years afterward those who could afford them paid good money to have a set of Waterloo teeth. It's said the name became a kind of brand, so much so that people still purchased and wanted Waterloo Teeth even when the supply had long been exhausted. The American Civil War proved a boon to dentists and those who wanted to smile and eat. Barrels filled with teeth now began crossing the Atlantic in the opposite direction. Dental supply catalogs in England and America advertised Waterloo Teeth throughout the 1860s. And for years after the war, men and women in France and England smiled with the dead teeth of American soldiers, a row of ivory tombstones fixed within their mouths.

How does anyone leave a war behind them, no matter what war it is, and somehow walk into the rest of his life?

I was flown on a C-130 with the rest of my unit to Kuwait and a huge canvas tent where our battalion sat shoulder to shoulder in long rows, an odd checklist given to each of us along with a pencil, a bored sergeant walking up and down the aisles imploring us to place a checkmark in any applicable boxes, barking with a disaffected voice woven from boredom and repetition over the high-n-tights of the battalion skulls arrayed before him – 'If you have seen any dead bodies, place a mark in the box next to *dead bodies*; if you have seen dismembered bodies, a-gain, place a mark in the box next to *dismembered bodies.*'

This is when Bruzik leans forward in the row to tell all of us in the squad, 'Check every box, men. Check 'em all. The military is going to hold you accountable for what you write on this paper and you just don't know what you might remember later, but can't remember now.'

He sees the look in my eyes. He knows, and I know it, too – that it's not the things I've seen that I'm worried about, exactly. I know that, when I leave the tent, tens of thousands, perhaps hundreds of thousands, perhaps even millions, of dead people will begin leaving the tent and following us home. And the wounded, and the maimed, and the traumatised, and the frightened, and the shattered, and the shivering, and the bruised, and the broken, and the disfigured. The ruined world will call its home inside of me. And all of them will follow us to our planes and board with us. They'll walk through the streets of America, through my home town, standing in my backyard late at night, sometimes, sitting at the foot of the bed to witness my wife and me curled together in dream.

Bruzik can see the look of it as I stare at the sheet in front of me. He pauses, and then says a few words about Miller – Miller, who killed himself in Mosul. 'That's one of the things I'm gonna have to take home. Seeing him after. You know? Seeing him like that. That's what I'll have for the years to come, brother. But let me tell you – that's the best we can do. We can't carry more than the ruck on our back. That's the best we can do.'

116

What happens when you come home?

A band of Vietnamese warriors, centuries back, returning to their village after a battle. Their loved ones gather everyone from the village and head out in the direction of the returning warriors. The warriors are not allowed to return to their village until the ritual is completed, until those they loved meet them in the jungle to wash and clean their bodies of all that war had placed upon them. They have to be given back their names just as their warrior names have to be returned to the tribe, given to the work of memory, history. The warriors lay down their weapons while the villagers sing a song to greet them. Their bodies are washed. Washed until the warriors shone with the light that water brings to the skin that carries it.

117

When my brigade returned from Iraq, platoons and companies and whole battalions stood in formation on a grassy parade field at Ft Lewis, Washington. Crisp uniforms. Fixed bayonets. Flags unfurled. The Colonel gave a speech as family and friends and reporters watched from the aluminum bleachers. It was difficult to hear him from where I stood, even over the loud-speakers. He was a small and distant man, and as he delivered his speech, one bromide at a time, I thought his men were equally small in his own eyes. Distant figures echoed by the pine trees beyond. He paused. A moment of silence, and he read the names of those who did not make it back.

He completed the list and continued on with his speech, and I realised that he hadn't spoken the name of Private First Class Bruce Miller. A young man from New Jersey who wrote poetry and wanted to become a lawyer one day.

The entire brigade stood there in the clipped grass, motionless. The Colonel drifted further and further away on a speech of heroes and sacrifice and nation-building. A soldier locked up his knees and passed out, instantly pissing his pants while slumping forward and cutting the man in front with his bayonet. I listened to the bugle play. We rendered our salute to the colors and tears welled in the eyes of those standing in the bleachers with their hands over their hearts. I did nothing to deserve the notes that rang from that horn.

118

I fly to Cape Town, Nairobi, Kampala. I fly to Istanbul, Bangkok, Hanoi. Budapest. Belgrade. Derry/Londonderry. The list expanding as the years go by. Kraków. Göteborg. Tokyo. Rome. In each place, beauty. And without exception – war.

I give a poetry reading in Liverpool and visit inmates at Walden Prison. After the reading in the prison chapel, one of the prisoners leans forward in his chair, his left leg slightly bouncing as he asks, 'So – how many did you kill?'

I pause. The guards at the back stop jangling their key rings when I look at the man and say, 'About 1.2 million.'

Outside Brčko in northern Bosnia, not far from the Sava River, I'm standing where my NATO base stood a decade before, at the turn of the millennium, but has now disappeared.* A local taxi driver, Denis Selimbasic, smokes a cigarette beside me. He gives me a moment to visualise the berms which once formed the base perimeter of Camp McGovern. Rows of sea huts, the Wagon Wheel Café, the front gate, the ammo point – all of it gone. Small tree saplings sprouted up in the storm-darkened soil.

In a sense, I'm witnessing the erasure of a kind of set design, the dismantling of a stage treatment. It's satisfying and troubling at the same time: to see how the landscape pulls the vestiges of war under and replaces them with a monument of cypress and birch. In the decades and centuries to come, the violence that took place in the Balkans will be forgotten and passed over by many, footnoted in historical texts, perhaps, or mentioned in a paragraph sketching the atrocities of the twentieth century.

Still, war is far more relentless, far more patient, than this. Just as the body is known to 'weep' glass shards and embedded

---

* I was stationed with the 10th Mtn Division out of Ft Drum, New York, at Camp McGovern as part of the NATO forces in Bosnia-Herzegovina (1999–2000).

debris long after an injury has scarred and healed over, war shares its deep reserves of trauma, with those searching for it or not.

Denis exhales the smoke from his lungs while offering the pack of Drina Special Filters. The grass, meanwhile, in thin clusters and solitary blades, resumes its work around us.

120

The *Maarten Jakob*, a Dutch fishing trawler, pulls up its morning haul of North Sea cod and gulls cry out in the air above, their bright bodies banking in sharp turns around the slight pitch and fall of the boat. Roughly 100 km west of Ijmuiden, the crew of the *Maarten Jakob* look on as the swollen net pours water over the deck and the main winch lowers the catch down to them.

It's not uncommon for fishermen in the North Sea to bring up ordnance from the Second World War in their nets. Still, there's no way of knowing when death arrives. There's no way of knowing that two of them, dead before they hit the water, will be thrown into the blue air by the force of the blast. A third man is about to die on the deck itself, a bomb from the 1940s arriving from the cold dark to discover him in the year 2005.

It happens the world over, because pain is often a creature of
great patience. This is a portion of the wisdom that the legless
man in Phnom Penh has earned. This is why he grips my hand,
hard, and won't let it go. It's the simple gesture, this wordless
moment that I'll return to in the years to come, thinking –

Such patience the mine has, waiting
under a canopy of years, the boy who placed it

now a taxi driver in Battambang,
a man who might offer you a cigarette

and a light, a keen believer in secrets,
whose great fear lies in knowing

all things are undone within us,
given time. Like this clockwork of metal.

This unwinding conversation
with a Tuesday morning from long ago.

All the days you may have forgotten
somehow made crucial and meaningless both –

just days, just a life, just your life
brought to this green place, the sunlight

edging the world around you in gold,
the way you'd like to be remembered, perhaps,

the green world you pass through
lit with fire, as if the landscape itself

loved you, brushing your face gently
with its many leaves.

122

Countries are touching countries and I cross over from one
to another, trying to shake the past and find a world I can
live in.

123

You want boom boom hot fuck nasty girl?

    That's what the pimp asks after I pay the moto-remorque
driver at the entrance to the Night Market in Siem Reap,

Cambodia. An old man smokes a rolled cigarette outside the nearby 6-Eleven store, thankful for the boredom of the evening, while the night's insects spiral their way down from the sodium lights above.

I half expect him to speak to me, his voice crackling like an old song dialed up from forty years ago. And although he says nothing, we both know that as the stone faces at the Bayon temple stare out from the eighth century, the Khmer Rouge pass under their gaze, their *kramas* hung loose around their throats, dew in the trigger housing, the year 1972 searing itself into their hands and onto their tongues. Still, the stone faces remain silent. They listen to the birds in the high trees before dawn.

The helicopter lifts off the tarmac at Phnom Penh. In the darkness, it flies low over the Tonle Sap. The door gunner – a Frenchman who, decades later, will insist to me that he was *not* a mercenary – considers the moonlight boiling up through the water below. Ahead, the Khmer Rouge lie bivouacked in the ruins. The M60 rests oiled and charged in its mount and the Frenchman knows that bullets will soon rise from the earth to greet him and he will be deep in the hunt for souls.

It's what the old man remembers now as he rolls another cigarette and sits beside me at the 6-Eleven. The sound of that helicopter riding over the waters. The low *thwap-thwap-thwap-thwap* of the rotorblades spinning – one of the sounds of death, the machine gun's prelude. The impassive faces staring from their fixed stations within the temples. Soldiers running along narrow paths, leading most to damp holes in the earth.

The creeper vine pulling them under.

124

When I came home, I saw America being America. I watched England soldier on. A long line of soy vanilla lattes, caramel macchiatos with extra caramel drizzled on top. Tapping broken fragments of language to one another on the bright screens in their hands. Plastic palm trees swaying overhead. An uptempo jazz track playing through tiny speakers mounted just under the splay of light green fronds.

125

I drank white mochas with a layer of whipped cream. I tapped words onto my own bright screen. And as I did so, I considered the British soldier hanging from a ceiling beam in Kentish Town. I recognised the artillery officer's body floating past early morning kayakers in the Mersey estuary, the smoke from Scouse fumestacks drifting over. Just as it happens in

America. The veteran steps away from the chair and the rope does its work. Pills swallowed with whiskey or coconut rum under a bulb of crackling filament. In Detroit, in San Jose, in New Brunswick, in Roanoke, the same. Ice cubes clinking in the glass. Men and women remove their dog tags and step into the bathtub, the process of cleaning the apartment made much easier for those who arrive after it's done. Thoughtful. Considerate. A pistol or rifle barrel positioned inside the cavity of the mouth. The pad of the thumb depressing the safety. The fine series of lines which form the fingerprint placed gently on the curved metal of a trigger in its cold housing.

126

I remember my mother asking, 'So what pills, if you don't mind, do you have to take, honey?'

127

High-altitude drones continue their nightly patrols out of earshot above. Their onboard cameras zoom in – *click* – and pull back.

Zoom in – *click* – and pull back.

In Lexington, Kentucky, where it's 2012, Jenny discovers one of my relatives, Kurt, out in the street again, sleepwalking. A long row of spaced-out street lights flare sodium orange in a fine mist, the way his meds appear lined up on the bathroom counter each week. And Jenny says, 'Are you cold, honey?' when he looks at her. He shakes his head slowly, his eyes gazing down the road to where the blacktop disappears into darkness. 'Is it your sergeant again?' she asks.

'Yeah.'

She slides her fingers over Kurt's palm until they interlock with his own. She leans into him and traces the large purple heart tattooed on his biceps, traces the fine lettering of the dead sergeant's name, inked in cursive.

Jenny knows the bullets will start soon, as they always do. After the hydrocodone, after the Seroquel, after the cocktail is topped off with a benzodiazepine, Klonopin, Kurt will drift into what he sometimes calls the night's blue hours, oh-dark-thirty. That's when the RPGs fly overhead, when muzzle flashes and tracer rounds erase the city they live in, the rivers and mountains, all of Kentucky, gone. The sergeant's body lies on the road. The voices of Iraqis and Americans swirl around them in the darkness. Bullets chip and ping off the asphalt. The stars dust down over the soldiers as they run for cover.

At night, when she lies next to Kurt, she knows they are lying next to his dead sergeant, too. And Kurt has picked up his M16. He slides his Kevlar back on, adjusting the chin strap. And Jenny doesn't say anything just yet. She doesn't want to startle him. She doesn't want to provoke an involuntary re-action, a moment when he might roll over on top of her and begin choking her to death by some instinct of combat. So when he's fired through his first magazine, Jenny offers the next thirty rounds to him.

On that desolate road in the darkness, at a checkpoint somewhere south-east of Mosul and beside the winding curves of the Tigris River, Jenny wonders if families huddle together in the farmhouses nearby. She wonders if some of them have begun to wander out to this moment the way she has – to talk to their men, to lie down beside them as they fall, to help them somehow, if they can, as they crawl forward and fire at the Americans in the road.

129

About an hour's train ride south of Stockholm, Soud stands in front of an easel on the second story of the Iraqi community center where he teaches art, in a part of town known locally as Mesopotalje, or Little Mesopotamia. It's Saturday. His students left hours ago. The sun went down. He eats the dinner his wife wrapped in aluminum foil and placed in his backpack before he set off on his bike this morning. The paint will come to him, he thinks. The colors, the bright surfaces, the places where shadows lean and pool. Figures will appear. They will move and gesture. They will shift their weight and demand great patience.

For now, the canvas remains blank. A kind of whispering he must listen to for as long as it takes. He thinks the American soldier he spoke with earlier today has already met with psychologists at the clinic. Implements assemble themselves in his mind when he considers the clinic. Soldier's questions. A detention cell. Hoods and waterfalls of blue shift quickly into the naked forms of men lying prostrate on cold prison floors, rectal thermometers removed for the reading of the body's core temperature, which must fall within regulations and guidelines that are lost somewhere in a honeycomb of secret prisons shifting the world over.

Fragments. Flashes of light. Pieces only.

He paints a broken tree rising into a broken city.

Parts of windows. Parts of doors. The hard flat world in profile.

Lined edges of jawbones. Curved signatures of eyes, staring.

When I fly back to the States, a process that takes years and years, I sit in a window seat and sleep on a soft blue pillow the color of early morning light. The wars continue as I get married, drive from California to Florida, move from one ocean to another. The wars continue as I watch the snowfall in Lake Tahoe, as I climb into the Anasazi cliff dwellings north of Santa Fe, as Ilyse and I sit behind home plate on opening day, my wife and I watching C. C. Sabathia deliver the first pitch of a thriller my Yankees will lose in the last inning.

I fly home, repeatedly. Wheels up and wheels down. The other passengers clapping for any service members onboard when the flight attendant prompts them to do so. Their applause like the sound of small arms fire in the distance. I dream with my head against the starboard side and I wake thirsty.

There are bombs from the Second World War in the subsurface of London's Heathrow airport. A bomb was found in Schiphol airport, too. In Munich, a controlled blast of discovered ordnance recently froze Germans in place – the sound of the twentieth century ringing in their ears.

My wife and I drink tea from a pot of silver needle, a plate of scones with jam and butter sitting on the small table between us. We're inside the Cake Shop, 14 Bury Place, London, our legs exhausted from hours spent wandering the British Museum, entering the gates of archeology, the ruins of Nineveh, where I once spent a cold night shivering in newly fallen snow. For now, we sip hot tea and read.

No one seems to notice the de-mining teams working their way through the bookstore, through the crowded chairs and tables in the Cake Shop. I try to focus on the grains of sugar dissolving into our cups of tea. There are teams in the British Museum, too, carefully walking forward among the ruins and searching for the explosives that lie in wait there. In the alleys of London. In Russell Square. Waterloo Station. Just as they do in the cities and small towns of America, the bomb disposal units working tirelessly and without notice, marking the sites, annotating the distributions of lethal ordnance, donning bomb suits and unspooling one another on white tethers, pausing to catch their breath before kneeling down to disengage the hard physics set before them.

Many years later, I arrive in Florida. My wife and I make love in sheets the color of rare wine. As we kiss and roll over in bed, in the heat of our bodies joined together, her legs folding over my lower back, a nurse wheels a shallow-breathing veteran into our bedroom – a man with pellets from a shotgun lodged in his brain, the surgeons following behind and standing over his gurney, whispering how they might proceed. The nurse motioning for more gurneys to be wheeled in.

Journalists shuffle into our bedroom and wait patiently for us to finish making love. They want me to talk about suicide. They want me to talk about hand-to-hand combat – something I really know nothing about. They want a modern definition for the word *obscenity* and the word *slaughter*. If that's what drives the veterans to kill themselves, well, then that makes sense, they say. The horror and all. That makes sense.

And they wait for us to finish making love. The journalists with their questions. The surgeons whispering over their critical patients. The dead in their bathtubs. The dead with their mouths given to foam. The dead strung from ropes under cones of light.

I sometimes think of a conversation between myself and the man in Mosul with a rocket launcher resting on his shoulder – the way the banyan trees stare for years across a stretch of sky. Wordless. I sometimes imagine him lying in bed with his wife, who curls beside him the way my wife does now, dreaming somewhere far off within the mysteries of the universe.

Some nights, late, late at night, a great horned owl swoops in to roost in the branches of the tree outside. It calls out with its other-worldly voice. Somewhere between a state of wakefulness and a state of dream, I am above the desert where the Kuwaiti border meets Saudi Arabia. The drone looks down on the regiments and battalions long buried in the dunes and trench systems and bunker complexes there. Some of them must have heard the long-range, high-altitude bombers hunting for them high in the earth's atmosphere. The bomb-bay doors opening to release explosives left over from the Vietnam War, bombs not even meant for them, and yet, here they were, falling.

Concussion bombs. The men caught in the open ground. The bombs exploding at a pre-set distance above them – shock waves reverberating their deadly physics onto the Iraqis below. And the man who fired the RPG across the traffic circle – maybe he thought about this, too. Maybe he thought of his own father lying in the dunes, bones shattered by the detonation's waves pressing down, his internal organs failing, his eyes staring up at a brilliant sky, or a star field at night.

134

Maybe it isn't that it's so difficult coming home, but that home isn't a big enough space for all that I must bring to it. America, vast and laid out from one ocean to another, is not a large enough space to contain the war each soldier brings home.

And, even if it could – it doesn't want to.

135

My unit trained to fight in Iraq, in part, by conducting field exercises out in the high desert country near Yakima, in eastern Washington State. I remember an overcast day, my squad on the slope of a low ridge covered in dead, waist-high grass. Some of the men sat in the grass and drank from the tubes of their CamelBaks. My machine-gunner, Barnes, a self-proclaimed Flori-baman, said, 'God-damned if it don't ever cool off in the daytime here. Jesus H, Sergeant, I swear – it's hotter'n a French whore in N'Orleans, even with the cloud cover.'

A soft-shelled Humvee drove up and parked with its wheels

turned at a hard angle, ready to drive off in a hurry. A thin, older man stepped out from the passenger side and half waved to us in a gesture that said 'No need to get up, men' – even though none of the guys had moved from their stations in the grass. He was an unexpected sight: dressed in jeans and a light windbreaker, dark sunglasses and an army baseball cap. The man introduced himself as Colonel Wardynski. Smiling and shaking my hand, the colonel asked how we were getting on and went on to explain that they were developing an online computer game for the army and that they'd like to 'grab audio' and get some video of us, if we didn't mind. The colonel's driver, leaning against the Humvee in his green and pressed Battle Dress Uniform, lit up a cigarette and stared in full boredom at the landscape rolling into the distance. In the middle of nowhere, 'bum fuck Egypt' as Barnes often put it, the colonel's request and presence seemed like a bizarre intrusion, as if we'd suddenly discovered ourselves on a television game show, part of some elaborate hoax. Dog-tired, salt-crusted, most of the men down to their final few cigarettes or worse, we stared at the colonel and didn't really know what to say.

'*America's Army*. That's what it's called, men. And we're going to put you inside the game. You'll be one of the characters.'

As acting squad leader during the field exercise, I was asked to step away from the squad and into the burned summer grass while Colonel Wardynski slowly filmed me with a hand-held video camera. He didn't use a tripod. He simply aimed the camera at my face and upper torso before lowering the camera down to my boots. He repeated this process for each side view and for the back. He then held a digital recorder near my chest to record me depressing my squad radio, asking me to say a few common phrases into the mic. I pressed the mic and said, 'Bravo Team, move!' and 'What's your status? Give me an up.' I said, 'Suppressive fire!' and 'Talk the guns!' and 'Roger that.'

I've thought back to that day in Yakima where Barnes later stood atop a ridge, arms fully extended with his M249 squad automatic weapon hanging from its shoulder sling, saying to the sun dying on the western horizon, to all of us and to no one at all, 'From this day forward and for all time, I proclaim everything that I can see, from here to the Pacific Ocean, as the Land of Barnes.' And I've wondered about the digital version of me, Sgt Turner, wandering through the wreckage of war, year after year, calling out to the others in the game, shooting at blurry enemy combatants, crawling through the grass, running through the ruined streets of unnamed cities and villages, scanning through the scope of my rifle for the silhouettes framed by windows across a digital river. I've wondered at the things I've seen there, the things I've done, the soldiers beside me moving forward when I say 'Bravo Team, move!' The Bravo Team leader calling out to me for years and years, moving his team forward and deeper into the shit every time I tell him to 'Move, move, move!'

At 3 a.m., when I've finally drifted off to sleep after curling up with my wife in our bed in Florida, someone in Saginaw or Portsmouth or Kettleman City toggles Sgt Turner forward into the firefight, the radio squelch unmistakable before my voice cuts in, eyes scanning the pixelated alley ahead, faded laundry hanging out to dry on the balconies above while a medic in a nearby room treats the wounded that the squad and the game will soon leave behind. And when Sgt Turner takes a knee, the battlefield assumes a certain calm. Flies buzzing. A dog barking in the distance. It is a world where the wounded don't bleed and the orphaned don't wail out in anguish and confusion.

And the enemy dead – they are left in their profound silence to remain face down on the hard soil they come from, not one of them rising from the broken clock of the body, as a ghost might do, to follow Sgt Turner through the streets and fields of this phantom world.

On Block Island, a tiny island shaped like a drop of water, the conductor of the sweat lodge explains the ceremony about to unfold. I stretch the corded muscles of my neck, fold one arm over my chest and brace the opposite hand above my elbow to stretch my triceps. Nerves. I listen to a description of the cardinal directions in relation to the symbolism of the lodge as thoughts pass overhead, restless, like reconnaissance planes.

It's a cold and windy April morning, a couple of hours past dawn, and the shifting winds blow through our hair and through the leaves around us with a musical rush. I'm barefoot, shivering a little in the damp orchard grass. Last night's rainfall has muddied the ground and left small pools of reflective water here and there. The wind and rain are slated to pick up as the day progresses. An understory of foliage, red clover and sea rocket forms a natural wall around the clearing where the lodge has been built. Cinnamon ferns and rockweed. Bulrush and sedge. All of it rising into viburnum, blackberry, autumn olive. The ground was carefully chosen.

About seven miles offshore, out into the Atlantic, from where the wind comes, a German submarine, *U-853*, rests on the ocean floor with its crew of fifty-five German sailors still manning their positions in an underwater grave. It was sunk by American forces in 1945, after Hitler's short-lived successor, Karl Doenitz, called for German units to cease fire and return home. Centuries earlier, in 1637, John Endicott landed on the shores of Block Island with an armed group of English colonists bent on killing the native men, women and children. When the killing stopped, fourteen members of the Niantic nation were dead (and all of their dogs shot) before the colonists burned wigwams and corn crops – thus initiating what turned into the Pequot War.

I've stripped down to a pair of shorts. Beside me is a gathering of strangers. We shiver and cross our arms to warm ourselves as we listen to the conductor. A line of cedar shavings marks the ground in a straight line from the circle of fire, where the sweat stones are given their necessary heat, to the opening of the sweat lodge itself. Smoke from the sacred fire shifts with the turning wind and blows into our faces. We squint and breathe in the ashy fragrance.

The lodge is a temporary dwelling, built over a series of tarps laid on the ground. A low framework of sturdy branches is lashed and intertwined together in the form of a dome covered in thick layers of blankets. The entrance is a simple rough blanket flap facing the east, toward sunrise, the direction of all beginnings. Inside, in the very centre of the lodge, a hole has been dug to hold the sacred and glowing stones which the fire keeper carries from the bonfire outside using a set of deer antlers. Women sit in the northern half, men in the southern. The glowing stones are transferred from the fire keeper at the doorway and placed in the pit.

I crawl in and find a spot for myself, my eyes struggling to adapt to the heavy darkness. My ears attune themselves to each nuance of sound. Bodies shifting as they seek comfort and space. A cavern filled with slow, deep breathing. An occasional cough. The flap opens and a broken pane of morning light casts a pale haze into the lodge, just long enough for the transfer of another stone, the warmed bones of the earth, and then we are submerged into darkness again.

The sweat conductor sprinkles an offering of tobacco over the coals, which crackle and sizzle tiny bright embers, some quick to rise in flame and disappear, a fragrant incense of tobacco drifting down to all of us below. There is an atmosphere of immediacy and pressure – the heavy layer of blankets above combine with the undulating contours of the earth beneath me to create the sense of a living, breathing organism, ribs of the whale I cannot ignore. A husk-rattle sounds its dry rain in the lodge, and as the sound of the rattle diminishes, the lodge conductor begins to chant, low and resonant, a sound deeply human at its core, a meditation that rises and then swirls slowly around the room as if the voice were sealing the edges of the lodge, passing over each of our bodies in the darkness.

When the drum begins, it's as if the earth's heart has been summoned through fiery stones into the world again, synchronous and tonal, an airy breath reverberating in the skin of the drum, each sound rising to the crest of its wave before easing into a downward glissando. And then a crash of water on stone – a ladle pouring a clear waterfall over the pile of stones. An instantaneous column of steam rises to the apex of the dome, where it curls and folds into itself while evenly spreading out over the lodge before descending in an undulation that comes, even now, even at its most expected moment, as a pure shock of heat. A wave of heat that wholly focuses the mind toward the heat itself. It becomes an entity all its own. My chest tightens and the long smooth muscles of my body tense themselves in an instinctual reaction to the overwhelming sensation, as if the body were retreating in the face of some essential truth. Dry, oppressive heat. I try to breathe, but the stony air is harsh and mineral and made of the furnace long held within the caverns of the earth.

And again the crash of water on stone. Another wave of heat rolling over. The cool liquid sound of the ladle dipping into the water. A sound of medicine. Then the pause, the slight delay, the deliberation in darkness followed by the next crash, the next column of steam, the next wave. I lose count of it all. Sweat slides in heavy beads from my forehead and temples. My body is covered in a gloss of sweat. I sluice my hair back with my palm, wipe my face with the back of my hand. Sweat immediately pearls on my upper lip again. And

I realise – heat draws the ocean from our bodies. It reduces us to mineral and bone. Desiccation. Heat demands that the desert reveal itself.

From the West

Now, high overhead, tiny figures begin to rappel down the rare filaments of the imagination, along fibers of the optic nerve and down into the hippocampus, into the landscape of days.

Old friends and strangers pause to watch as each figure calls out, 'On belay,' before pushing off from the closed lid of the eye above, while some in the gathering crowd below rush forward to grab the ends of the lines, responding, 'Belay on.' Soldiers from my old platoon land on their feet, undo the corded rope from their snap-links, and stare at me for a moment through night-vision goggles.

They don't seem to recognise me at first. Then one turns to another, saying, 'It's Ghost 1–3 Alpha.'

'No shit. Sergeant T? That you?' says another.

I nod my head as they pass hand signals down the line and then fan out to take cover. They seem to be providing overwatch, or simply waiting for something to happen. There is a bone-colored camel in the distance. The sound of an owl calling out. This is when the ten-year-old Iraqi boy walks up and tells me, in halting English, that he will take me to the man I need to see. I follow the soft fall of his footsteps as he walks into the darkness of the world. I can feel the hard asphalt beneath my feet. I realise that the landscape has taken on a pale green aspect, a glaucous night-vision green, and that I must be wearing the goggles now, too. The small boy looks back over his shoulder and motions for me to continue forward. The boy's eyes are black stones. I hear voices in the distance, low and indistinct.

'*Jundee*,' the boy says. 'Look.'

The ruined car is to my left. Ruckled metal. Fluids pooling under a dead engine venting steam. Doc High speaks in Latin to a dying man lying prostrate on the road surface. And through night-vision goggles I see the dying man raise his head through obvious pain, his forehead punctured deep with the mark of a horsehoe; no, with an injury shaped like the bars of a prison – the signature of the wound I gave him so many years ago.

'Now,' the boy says to me. 'You must do this. Now.'

I'm not sure what it is I'm supposed to do. The man is dying, and has been dying for years, I think.

'My father,' the boy says to me, 'you start with him. There are many more after him.'

'Sergeant T,' Doc High says, getting my attention. 'I told him what I always tell him. I said – *The man who killed you is coming now. He'll take you to the next world.*'

* * *

The sweat conductor sounds the drum once then, a clear, ringing drumhead that opens my eyes to the darkness of the lodge just as the blanket flap announces the sunlit world outside in a flare of light. I roll over onto my side, wipe the sweat from my face and neck with a small hand towel and crawl in a clockwise direction to join the others in the bright air.

The wind announces itself over the entire surface of my body, as if the world were a motion of cool water, while I raise my arms toward the low clouds rolling overhead, stormy and wild. I feel as convoluted and gray as the clouds. I feel lighter than my body, which I recognise as a failed but beautiful instrument capable of so much more than I ever allow it. I can hear some of the others in the grass around me laughing, some whooping, some rotating their bodies and wheeling like pinwheels driven by the Atlantic.

After a few long pulls of water from a plastic jug, I follow them back into the lodge for the next round of heat and steam, the next round spent learning from the stones.

From the North

I'm sitting in the Emergency Waiting Room located far below the blue curving dome of my skull, down below the lamp-lit streets of the cerebellum, somewhere at the back of the brain where ambulances disappear beyond glassy hospital doors as they make their way into the night's cerebral fluid.

I'm eating chocolate pudding from a small plastic cup and it's bland, smooth, nearly tasteless. Hospital cafeteria food. The nurse at the night desk looks bored. She files her nails and blows the dust off their tips after every three or four passes of the emery board. Voices come and go on the intercom system. Some of them sound as if they were spoken years before, only just now arriving in the tiny cones of the speakers screwed into the ceiling. On the television stationed high up in the corner of the room, a documentary on whales has just finished and, after a brief commercial interruption, another documentary begins. A psychophysiologist discusses neural pathways and the coding processes of memory. The nurse at the desk waves a remote control at it and the channel switches to a black and white movie from the 1950s that I can't remember the name of.

My dead Uncle Paul sits next to me. His left arm sleeps in the white triangle sling he wore after the stroke. If I subtract all of the other sounds in the waiting room and beyond, I can hear the tiny metal valve snapping open and snapping shut inside his heart. Uncle Paul leans his head back and says, to me or maybe to the speakers in the ceiling above, 'Fuck, what I wouldn't do just to have one drag of a Marlboro.'

My younger brother, Chris, sits across from us. He laughs and then leans over to hand me a set of his X-rays. I hold them up to the fluorescent light and see the cancer he described over the phone, white erasures in the body's dark caverns, light in its deadly blare.

My mother walks through the rows of seats with my grandmother's urn cradled in her left arm, nestled on her hip the way a mother might carry a young child. My grandfather follows them both, leaning on his cane, smiling at everyone he passes. He stoops with a slightly bent back when he walks, which I mistake for the use of the cane at first – until I notice the tanks of the flamethrower strapped to his back.

My father has laid a mat out over by the water cooler. He's practicing a kata from our days in the dojo. One by one, the foes from his past approach to assault him and, in slow motion it appears, effortless and filled with grace, he hammer-fists them to the sternum, he knife-fists them, he wheel-kicks and elbows and he gathers in the centered *chi* which then spirals electric out through the points of his body in a light that sends each of his opponents reeling back into the void from which they came.

My wife, Ilyse, leans her head on my shoulder, now and then shifting her head so she might kiss the muscle shielding the cagework of bone over my heart. She draws the fingers of her right hand slow through my hair and it feels like cool water rolling down the smoothest face of stone.

She knows that my best friend, Brian Voight, will soon be arriving by ambulance. She knows that he's going to hand me jar after jar of the stage-IV fluid the doctors keep drawing from his body. Soon, I'll need to get crates to collect them all in.

Doc High calls to me from near the wide doors that lead to the surgical theater beyond. 'Sergeant Turner,' he says.

I don't move. He says something to the man on the gurney, something in Latin, I think, then pauses to look at me over his shoulder. 'He's dying, Sergeant Turner. Are you going to help? I can do the compressions, but I need you to breathe for him.'

The small metal hinge in my uncle's heart keeps ticking beside me. My cousin Kyle, his own dead sergeant from 2003 sitting next to him, says to me, 'I'm telling you, one soldier to another, no matter what the grief, its weight, we are obliged to carry it.'

And as the old western on the TV in the corner drones on, Doc High says, 'Sergeant T – bandages. We need bandages.'

The drum sounds.

At first, I can think of nothing other than the heat. I remember how we'd been instructed not to worry and panic, that we'd be okay, that the heat would seem too much, too crushing, and more. That if we felt it was simply more than we could take we could just carefully crawl out and breathe in the air outside, regain our composure, join in the next round.

The stones are given more water, a cascading fall of fluid that crashes and hisses into the bones of the earth. The very

physical body of the steam greets me, though I dread its approach,
the pure heat of it drawing closer and closer in the darkness of
the lodge, where my imagination returns to lead me.

From the East

     I'm wearing pajamas and standing in the backyard
          with a shovel. Florida. Home.

     Moonlight on the Spanish bayonets. Moonlight
          on the waters of Lake Adair.

                *

     A shovel in the earth, blade by blade, as the dead
          line up in silence under the lime trees.

                *

     Their heads, steaming. My wife brings coffee.
          We pause, two figures in the grass.

                *

     Each hole measures roughly 6´ x 6´ x 4´.
     Each hour the moon filling them with light.

                *

     Some hand me a copy of their depositions.
          They point out my signature,

     a curl and fall of black ink,
          and below that: Sgt Turner.

The soil gathers in cold mounds beside the graves.

No one knows why, an old man tells me. *No one.*

We should ask their names, my wife says, *and write*
   them down. If not for us then for those who come
   after.

We guide them to the cold earth below, saying
   Careful now and *Here, let me help you down.*

I ask if they'd like water.
   Something to eat.

If they'd like to say something
   before the earth comes down.

They turn their heads toward Mecca
   when the time comes, listening

for the call to Azan, for any voice carried
   over the rooftops of the world.

We lift our feet and press down. Tamp the soil.
Stand to the side when their loved ones mourn.

*

For each fresh grave, a television for a headstone.
Row after row of Technicolor screens.

*

Curved glass and tubes glowing within. By dawn,
 the movies begin to play. *They Were*

Expendable. Sands of Iwo Jima,
 The Longest Day and *The Green Berets.*

*

We say *Let's see what Starlight-Starbright has to say.*
We say *What happens now?* and *Hang, Fire!* to each
 other.

*

We say *He bought the farm, Sir, but*
 He took a lot of them with him.

We say *Hell, we're still alive* and
 God willing and the river don't rise.

*

We listen to the actors
 with their hard-earned lines.

We repeat them, shovel by shovel,
 John Wayne Saturdays for all.

*

The drum sounds.

After another walk through the wind and the rain-soaked grass outside, I re-enter the darkness of the lodge and lie down. Rattles shake and singing fills the space, drums return, reverberating in their circular wave above us as we all lie with our backs on the earth and our faces anticipating the heat to come.

I have the distinct feeling that I'm not lying down at all. The earth has become a cool and uneven wall that I stand against for support.

Water crashes into stone. I call out to the stone, and the stone calls back.

From the South

Brilliant tracers line the winter sky, meteors arcing and burning through the upper atmosphere and continuing down to where the silhouettes open their arms to gather them in, Ilyse at my side, hand in hand, one stream of light after another coming down, and I realise we're witnessing a vast dispensary, a showering of pharmaceuticals, the prescriptions falling one after the other, antidepressents and antipsychotics, Risperdal, Seroquel, Geodon, Abilify, Adderall and Dexedrine, lithium and codeine and volproic acid, amoxapine, Xanax, Tramadol hydrochloride, diazepam and lorazepam, Cymbalta, Celexa, Solvex and Tryptanol falling into the weekly dosage trays for former Sgt Gutierrez, former Specialist Cody, former army medic SSG Wallace, Lance Corporal Boudreau, former Chief Warrant Officer Vanderwalle, as well as my own father, grandfather, uncle, cousins, and me when the time comes, the trays filling day by day with capsules and lozenges in their proper milligram doses, though maybe they aren't pills at all, maybe if I look closer at the night sky the pills turn to tiny parachutists growing larger and larger as they near, the 173rd Airborne out of Vicenza in the airdrop north of Mosul, perhaps, then, no, they are hospital beds with white sheets drifting slowly down, their guide ropes the plastic tubing tethering each patient to IV bags and push meds of morphine, Dilaudid, Toradol, Ativan, Zofran and Protonix, blood thinners and potassium boosters, bag after bag of plasma, O positive, B negative, B positive, AB negative, and the universal donor O negative, the clipboards at the foot of their beds reading *gunshot* and *blast wound* and *acute head trauma*, the clipboards listing their patients' names, Akram, Alima, Boosah, Faruq, Jameel, Lala, Nura, Pazhman, Saarah, Taneen and Zelgai—

—And as we stand together under a twenty-first-century rain, I point off into the distance, to the past, or to the future, or to a dream, perhaps, there's no way of telling, but I point to where the first raid of the night is already in progress.

Ilyse wears felt slippers, dark flannel pajama bottoms with a series of hearts embroidered down her left thigh, a green pullover with a hood and drawstrings, her hands tucked into its pocket pouch to ward off the chill, and she's walking into Mosul, into the year 2004, into the war.

The soldiers of 1st Platoon look up at her as they pull security from a bent knee, each scanning the rooftops and windows of the neighborhood in their sector of fire. The lasers on their weapons form an infrared geometry only those with night-vision goggles can see. Some of them whisper into their bone mics, saying, 'Hey, is that Turner's wife?' and 'Yeah – I seen some crazy shit, man, but this is some *crazy ass shit.*'

Ilyse walks past their blocking position and turns the corner, where an infrared chem light glows invisible to the naked eye, before walking on down the suburban street. She can just barely hear the Blackhawks hovering patient in the night air, on station a few minutes out, a sound that is nearly indistinguishable from the low ambient noise of the city. They remain at the threshold of human hearing for the time being, but they'll circle directly overhead once the assault team breaches the front door. Ilyse has already passed the battalion medrev Stryker with its surgeon and crew inside, who drink coffee and whisper jokes to one another in the troop hold as the vehicle's engine idles in the dark. And now she's passing the lieutenant, the LT, with his radio man, Walker, who switches frequencies and gives the handset to the LT while thinking about the cigarette waiting for him back at the base.

A Phoenix beacon strobes undetectable by the naked eye from a rooftop opposite the target house. From that rooftop, the company sniper team watches Ilyse walking up the street to the target house and they whisper to each other, saying, 'You got eyes on?' and 'What the hell is she doing?'

There are several Iraqi men sleeping inside the target house. I saw some of their faces during the briefing hours earlier. We were given a list of names. I've told my soldiers the details. We've gone over the five-paragraph operation's order. I prepped the demo charges on a plywood table with Sgt Z back at the base. Cut equal lengths of det cord from a spool and laid them side by side on a long strip of double-sided tape. And it won't matter if the Iraqi men inside the quiet, two-story house know that the explosive reaction within det cord travels at about four miles per second, or that the firing impulse in the shock tube which ignites the det cord travels at roughly 6,500 feet per second. They'll bolt upright from under the covers of dream when the huge metal car gate is blown open at its center seam, bent inward toward the house with jagged, saw-toothed metal, as if the wide maw of steel had unhinged its jawbone and peeled back its lips to snarl at them with its rough-cut teeth. The logic centers of the brain will be overwhelmed and paralysed by fear and panic when the second charge blows in the front door and the overpressure within the closed house blows out all of the front windows.

I don't know what it's like to have killers at the door, but I know what it's like to be one of the men with a rifle coming in. Eyes dilated night-vision green. Adrenaline in the vein. My finger pulling the safety pin and waiting for the countdown. A detonator in my hand. My body connected to an imminent explosion. The night cracking open in my hands.

And none of this seems to faze Ilyse. She just keeps walking toward me, nodding a faintly visible greeting to Bosch and Fiorillo, to Sgt Z and the follow-on assault team, to all who have taken a knee and listened for the countdown. I've taken a knee beside Jax and my squad leader, who whispers the countdown to the blast over the radio. When he gets to '4', Ilyse kneels in front of me, smiling. And none of it makes any sense to me. The war. The detonator in my hand. My wife with a series of hearts embroidered on her thigh. The numbers called out over the radio. The city of Mosul.

She reaches out to unfurl my fingers gently from around the detonator, which she takes from my palm and hands to SSG Bruzik, who nods and doesn't say a word.

She helps me to my feet and holds my hand as we quietly step away from the squad kneeling beside the wall to the target house. 'Just come with me,' she says. 'This way.'

And as we walk down the street, red streams of laser lights articulate the night above us in infrared, as if describing an architect's planned ceiling – the concept of a ceiling unable to block out the night's dim star field above.

Ilyse says nothing as we move farther and farther away, the streets getting darker and darker until we come to a wall with a shower faucet gleaming in silver over our heads. I stare at the faucet head and wonder how it could be here and why someone would plumb a showerhead along a wall on a darkened Mosul street as Ilyse undoes the chin strap of my Kevlar helmet and places it on the sidewalk beside us. She leans my M4 against the wall and helps me shake off my flak vest with its heavy plates of body armor and pouches of spring-fed magazines.

The water from the showerhead is warm and I lean my head back into the stream of it when it switches on. She unlaces my combat boots and helps me slip them off. And I'm soaked now. Water has poured over the sandy pattern of my ACUs until they cling to my body with a color more like the color of shadows. As I think about how water might somehow wrap our shadows around us, how it might lift the darkness we carry through the world and drape it over our skin as we stand under the showerhead, she pulls the Velcro flaps loose and unbuckles my belt.

I finally see her. She has crossed the great fires in the country between us. My eyes shift focus, readjusting. The world regaining its light. As if dawn were somehow given to the far horizon, though it must be hours away. I can see her. The liquid curve of her eyes, shining, as she slides my desert top back over my shoulders and lets it fall at our feet. My pants fall to my ankles and I step out of them, pushing them into the darkness with a slide of my foot.

We kiss under the wide fall of water. And as we kiss, with a dark beauty on our tongues, she draws shampoo through my hair with her cool fingers. I close my eyes for a moment to take in the fragrance of jasmine and lemon, the perfume of her body underwater and the darkness fallen long after midnight. And as I slide the zipper of her hoodie down its shiny channel, I can see our shadows on the flickering walls around us. We seem to be floating, rising, transparent as smoke. I wipe the soap from my eyes and focus on the small lights in the distance. I realise they are no longer the street lamps near the university district of Mosul. These small lights shift and move, as candlelight moves in the rooms of lovers, as candles shine in our own bedroom, steam of the shower fogging the bathroom mirror, the bedroom windows beyond.

Sgt Turner is dead.

Some nights he walks the streets and alleys of Mosul, in the company of the dead. Others, he steps into the homes of the living, perches on the beds of lovers, and considers the world as it continues on.

Tonight, he sits in a cockpit situated in a portable connex, the connex mounted on a vehicle driving through a desert or bivouacked in a low wadi somewhere in the world. It's difficult to tell from inside of the vehicle. He leans back against a foam-cushioned swivel chair, each hand gripping the controls, his thumb on the safety, index finger over the trigger, with a bank of monitors arrayed before him, streams of remote data computed and digitised into analytics an air force officer considers while drinking from a twenty-ounce bottle of Mountain Dew at the desk behind him, near the door. Another officer sits in the chair beside him, typing away at the many letters and numbers printed on the keyboard in front of him. Targets on the dry erase board coded in red, blue, green, purple, black and brown. Small plastic flags in a metal canister below. Radio traffic breaking in through the squelch over the speakers and through their headsets. In-country language. Language from another time, he thinks. And the language from back in the world, the language he's listening for.

Sgt Turner flips a toggle switch to shift from black-hot to white-hot. Takes a swig of harsh coffee, flattened some by powdered non-dairy creamer spooned in. Then he lowers the nose of the Predator drone to drop down in altitude as the bird arrives on approach to the target. He watches the altimeter and checks the angle of the flaps as the rush of wind on the bird's nose begins to transpose into red numbers rising in the speed gauge before him. After checking the map coordinates, he levels out the drone and begins to bank north, north-west, as he sets the drone in a circuit around the target house in the darkness below.

Florida. College Park. A three-bedroom house in a suburban neighborhood. A small wood deck off the back of the home. A stand of trees. A front lawn sloping out toward an unmarked roadway where a few streetlights glow at intervals over the road. Cones of light appearing like round warm discs from the onboard cameras fixed in their stations high above. The drone well out of sight. Out of earshot. Sgt Turner conscious of the necessary standoff distance. His attention wholly given to the two bright forms sleeping side by side in the bedroom, curling into each other, near the back of the house. The heat and intensity of their bodies blurring one into another, the sheets and mattress forming a cool black border around them. Sgt Turner takes another swig of coffee as the drone banks and turns in another circuit around the target. He considers the landscape of dream constructing itself in that tiny room below.

He will continue to monitor the house like this, zooming in sometimes, switching camera angles and lenses, collecting data, checking his gauges, flight speed, altitude. Sgt Turner will watch as night turns to morning, as the sun circles the earth, as night returns, circuit by circuit keeping his watch, even when the cardinals begin to sing from the branches of the golden raintree in the front yard, even when the trumpet flowers fill with light.

He will maintain his standoff distance. He will steady his hand on the weapon systems at his disposal. He will monitor the heat signatures of the living. And, because Sgt Turner is dead, he will remain at his post.

There is nothing strange in this at all.

Notes

vi

'Too many lives go into the making of just one' is from Eugenio Montale's
poem, 'Summer' (translated by David Young, *Selected Poems*, Oberlin
College Press, 2004).

2

Cleaner, Lubricant, Preservative (CLP) – provides solvents to dissolve
firing residue and carbon, a coating of Teflon to aid lubrication, and
prevents rust. Similar to a short length of rope, a bore snake is sometimes used to clean inside the barrel of a weapon.

'known and suspected enemy targets' – in other words, if you can't see
those shooting at you, fire back at any place you think you'd hide were
the situation reversed.

The 'sight picture' is what a shooter sees when viewing a target through
the sights of his or her weapon. On some weapons, there is a front 'sight
post' which serves to guide or orient the sight picture for the shooter.

3

During the convoy briefing just prior to entering Iraq, we'd been taught
an easy mnemonic to help us identify and deal with the 'enemy': *See
an AK-47 – Shoot it.*

Meditations by Marcus Aurelius, translated by Gregory Hays (The
Modern Library, New York, 2003). The passage referenced here (*leaves
that the wind drives earthward*) is an instance of Aurelius quoting a
famous passage from Homer's *Iliad*.

4

The excerpted passage ('Facing us on the field of battle . . .') is from *The
Bhagavad Gita*, translated by Juan Mascaro, Penguin Books, 1962
(Chapter 1: 34, p. 6).

Mark Kellogg (1831–1876), of the *Bismarck Tribune*, was the first Associated Press reporter to be killed in the line of duty (while following Custer into battle).

5

This passage is in conversation with an oil painting by Soyama Sachihiko (1859–92) called *Aiming at the Target*.

11

Gruinard Island Anthrax Experiment: http://www.youtube.com/watch?v= TipB2gV1iyk and http://www.youtube.com/watch?v=ig1Cz2tdVjY

19

'Artillery hammers the evening from a distant base' is a very slight shifting and lifting of a line from Bruce Weigl's 'Burning Shit at An Khe' (from *Song of Napalm*, Atlantic Monthly Press, 1988).

22

Hesco barriers. This large barrier system, or gabion, is made of wire mesh and thick felt material filled with sand. The Hesco barrier was invented by Jimi Heselden, a coal miner and entrepreneur from Leeds, England. In a sense, Jimi Heselden saved my life.

24

The information in this section depends upon *Classical Poems by Arab Women: A Bilingual Anthology*, ed. Abdullah al-Udhari, Saqi Books, 1999.

30

The words 'father' and 'dad' are used throughout this book in reference to my stepfather, Marshall Turner, who raised me and has always had a tremendous influence on my life. My biological father is not referred to in this book, but it should be noted that he served honorably in the engine rooms and after-engine rooms of several navy ships, including the USS *Bridget* (a destroyer escort), the USS *Halsey-Powell* (a Fletcher-class destroyer) and the guided-missile cruiser USS *Providence* during the 1960s.

33

For a very detailed meditation on composition and philosophical underpinnings of dojos, see: *In the Dojo* by Dave Lowry (Weatherhill, 2006).

35

The Poor Man's James Bond by Kurt Saxon (Atlan Formularies, 1972).

37

Fake blood was created by mixing several ingredients, including: water, corn
syrup, flour, red food dye, and chocolate syrup. This recipe attempted to
replicate Kensington Gore (created and manufactured by the British
pharmacist John Tynegate in Dorset). Other make-up effects in *The War
That Time Forgot* were inspired by Tom Savini's work in *Dawn of the
Dead*, though done on a twelve-year-old's budget.

44

For more information on Freyja, see R. B. Anderson's *Norse Mythology*:
Myths of the Eddas (Kessinger Publishing, LLC, 2007, though originally
published by S. C. Griggs and Co., Chicago, 1884) and Helene A.
Guerber's *Myths of the Norsemen* (Barnes and Noble, 2006, though
originally published in 1909 by Georgo G. Harran & Company,
London).

46

Ice-cream article is from http://whatsforsupper-juno.blogspot.com/
2010/07/lightly-spiced-south-african-guava-ice.html

48

MRE stands for Meals Ready to Eat; these are the portable rations
consumed by US military personnel.

49

This section is after (and in some conversation with) Rick Moody's 'Boys'
from *Demonology* (Back Bay Books, 2002).

Poetry quotes in this section are from Fadhil Al-Azzawi's poem, 'Every
Morning The War Gets Up From Sleep' translated by Salaam Yousif,
Iraqi Poetry Today, ed. Saadi Simawe, King's College London, 2003.

50

On 21 December 2004, shortly after my unit left Iraq, the dining facility
at FOB Marez was attacked by a suicide bomber. Twenty-two were
killed and seventy wounded.

59

This section owes a great debt to Emiko Ohnuki-Tierney's *Kamikaze, Cherry Blossoms, and Nationalisms: The Militarization of Aesthetics in Japanese History* (University of Chicago Press, 2002) and *Kamikaze Diaries: Reflections of Japanese Student Soldiers* (University of Chicago Press, 2007).

64

'[T]he world is still only the world' is from 'Worldly Beauty' by T. R. Hummer (*Walt Whitman in Hell*, Louisiana State University Press, 1996).

The bells in this section refer to the bells intoned daily at the site of the explosion, as well as to Takashi Nagai's *The Bells of Nagasaki* (Kodansha International, 1994, translated by William Johnston).

During a visit to Hiroshima, I stood near the hypocenter of the bomb as excited school children took photos in front of a humble stone monument marking the location. One of the girls wore a shirt with this English phrase written on it: *I can stand under the same sky.*

65

The Third Marine Division (Infantry Journal Press, 1948), by First Lieutenant Robert A. Aurthur (USMCR) and First Lieutenant Kenneth Cohlmia (USMCR), proved useful throughout the writing of this book. My grandfather served in the 3rd Marine Division.

70

http://www.baseballagreatestsacrifice.com/biographies/muramatsn_yukio.html

My father would be stationed on Eniwetok Atoll just two decades later, occasionally swimming near scuttled tanks from the Second World War, tanks that still housed the skeletons of the men who died within them.

73

German translation by Melanie Stammbach of Zurich, Switzerland, and Anna Mageras.

78

In November, 2003, an American helicopter was shot down near Fallujah, killing fifteen and wounding more than twenty.

81

'Believe Everything', by The Dead Quimbys, was mixed and mastered at Moonlight Studios, 2012. Follow this link to hear a cut ('Trilogy') from the album performed by Brian Voight (guitars, songwriter, backing vocals), Russell Conrad (vocals, percussion), Darren Lowenthal (drums, percussion, backing vocals), Brian Turner (bass, trumpet, backing vocals): http://brianturner.org/sections/believe-everything/

82

'A damn sad thing' is a line from 'Graves in Queens' by Richard Hugo (*What Thou Lovest Well, Remains American*, W.W. Norton & Company, 1975).

108

Walterinnesia aegyptia. At least one or two baby cobras were killed on the ground floor in our small gym, the same floor where we slept.

118

Regarding the figure 1.2 million, see: http://www.theguardian.com/world/2007/sep/16/iraq.iraqtimeline

119

My brother-in-law, Roger Green, was a sergeant in an artillery unit out of Colorado that replaced us in the following rotation.

121

This poem is a variation on a poem originally published as 'The Fire Flame Tree' in the *Alahambra Poetry Calendar* (2011).

128

'The stars dust down . . .' is a slight shifting and lifting of a line from 'A Far Galaxy' by Garrett Hongo (*River of Heaven*, Knopf, 1981).

136

'[T]houghts pass overhead, restless, like reconnaissance planes' is from 'The U.N. Headquarters in the High Commissioner's House in

Jerusalem' by Yehuda Amichai (*The Selected Poetry of Yehuda Amichai*, University of California Press, 1996).

'The boy's eyes are black stone' is a line slightly altered from Martin Espada's poem 'Black Islands' (in *The Republic of Poetry*, W.W. Norton, 2006).

No matter what the grief, its weight, we are obliged to carry it' is a line from 'For the Sake of Strangers' by Dorianne Laux (*What We Carry*, Boa Editions Ltd, 1994).

'*What happens now? . . . Hang, Fire!*' – this dialogue is from *The Green Berets* (Warner Bros.–Seven Arts, 1968).

'I call out from the stone, and the stone calls back' is a line from *The Book of Nightmares* by Galway Kinnell (Houghton Mifflin Company, 1971).

'We seemed to be floating, rising, transparent as smoke' is a line from 'Forgiven' by Corrinne Clegg Hales (*To Make It Right*, Autumn House Press, 2011).

Acknowledgements

Sections of this book have appeared in the *Virginia Quarterly Review* ('My Life as a Foreign Country', Fall 2011) and in the *Connecticut Review* ('Firebase Eagle', Fall 2010). Many thanks to Peter Catapano at the *New York Times*, Victoria Pope and Peter Miller at *National Geographic*, and to Ted Genoways – who challenged me to write this book and helped me to grapple with the material from the very beginning.

My editor at Jonathan Cape, Alex Bowler, took the raw blocks of language I gave him and helped me to shape them into the book you now hold in your hands. He's proof that the word *editor* can be synonymous with the word *artist*.

I'm grateful for the steadfast friendship, belief, and patience of Samar Hammam, who has seen this project through from beginning to end (and, truly, for several years before that – expecting a novel). Samar has offered her keen ear to each draft along the way. Likewise, I'd like to thank Alison Granucci, with Blue Flower Arts, for the profound and lasting impact she's had on my life and for the doors she continually opens to the greater world.

To Donald Anderson, Benjamin Busch, Kelle Groom, Patrick Hicks, Col. Tom McGuire, Pete Molin and Alexi Zentner – I give thanks for their generosity of spirit and the deep attention they offered to multiple drafts of this book. I'd especially like to thank my dear friend, Stacey Lynn Brown, for her insights, suggestions and close reading of this work.

I'm grateful to the Lannan Foundation; Margeret Mihori, Christopher Blasdel, and Manami Maeda with the Japan-United States Friendship Commission; the International House Librarian in Tokyo – Rie Hayashi; the Amy Lowell Traveling Fellowship; United States Artists; the William Joiner Center for the Study of War and Social Consequences; Matt O'Donnell at From the Fishouse (www.fishousepoems.org); Neil Astley at Bloodaxe Books; Carey Salerno at Alice James Books; and the Kerouac Project of Orlando, for support, guidance and encouragement.

Portions of this book were written in Albania, Bosnia-Herzegovina, Croatia, Greece, Ireland, Japan, Macedonia, Portugal, Thailand, Turkey and the United Kingdom, as well as in the Moore family bungalow (Donaghadee, Northern Ireland), the Artist's Suite at the Betsy (Miami Beach, Florida), the Federal Association of Globetrotters bar (Belgrade, Serbia), the Bright Lotus Lodge (Phnom Penh, Cambodia), the

Metropole Hotel (Hanoi, Vietnam), and on the 3rd Floor Cancer Unit at Winter Park Memorial Hospital in Orlando, Florida.

To the many friends who've made this work possible, in one way or another – Tony Barnstone, Shannon Beets, Jeff Bell, Kevin Bowen, Matt Cashion, Russell Conrad, Patsy Garoupa, Corrinne Clegg Hales, Nathalie Handal, Lee Herrick, Devin High, Garrett Hongo, T.R. Hummer, Kwang Ho Lee, Haider Al-Kabi, Maura Kennedy, Declan Meade, Dunya Mikhail, Sadek Mohammed, Sarah Mustafa, Soheil Najm, Oliver de la Paz, Suzanne Roberts, Mike Robinson, June Saraceno, Jared Silvia, Ryan Southerland, Matthew Sweeney, Bill Tuell, Bruce Weigl, Ofer Ziv, and to those whose names I cannot write here (due to the possibility of danger to their lives or to their loved ones) – *thank you*. If I have forgotten anyone in the process it is simply because there are so many who have given so generously of their time, talent and energy, and for that I will always be grateful.

To those I served with – thank you for making the rest of my life possible.

My thanks also to those who didn't kill me – whether by mistake or by choice. I owe my days, in part, to you.

My love and thanks to friends and family both near and far.